VICENTE SILVA AND HIS FORTY BANDITS

Manuel Cabeza de Baca in ceremonial attire.
(Courtesy of the Cabeza de Baca Family)

VICENTE SILVA AND HIS FORTY BANDITS
HIS CRIMES AND RETRIBUTIONS

MANUEL CABEZA DE BACA

*in a New Translation
from the Spanish*

by
DOLORES GUTIÉRREZ MILLS
and
CARMEN CABEZA DE BACA PACE

SUNSTONE
PRESS
SANTA FE

Sunstone books may be purchased for educational, business, or sales promotional use.
For information please write: Special Markets Department, Sunstone Press,
P.O. Box 2321, Santa Fe, New Mexico 87504-2321.
Printed on acid-free paper

∞

eBook 978-1-61139-677-5

Library of Congress Cataloging-in-Publication Data

Names: C. de Baca, Manuel, author. | Gutiérrez Mills, Dolores, 1938-
translator. | Cabeza de Baca Pace, Carmen, 1921- translator.
Title: Vicente Silva and his forty bandits : his crimes and retributions /
Manuel Cabeza de Baca in a new translation from the Spanish by Dolores
Gutiérrez Mills and Carmen Cabeza de Baca Pace.
Description: Santa Fe, NM : Sunstone Press, [2022] | Summary: "This story
of the reign of terror and the crimes perpetrated by Vicente Silva and
his forty bandits during the early 20th century in the northern New
Mexico town of Las Vegas in this new translation by descendants of the
author is a tribute to the resilience of the people of Las Vegas during
those troubled times"-- Provided by publisher.
Identifiers: LCCN 2022011115 | ISBN 9781632933706 (paperback) | ISBN
9781611396775 (epub)
Subjects: LCSH: Silva, Vicente, 1845-1893. | Brigands and robbers--New
Mexico. | New Mexico--History--1848-
Classification: LCC F801 .C26 2022 | DDC 978.9/04--dc23
LC record available at https://lccn.loc.gov/2022011115

WWW.SUNSTONEPRESS.COM
SUNSTONE PRESS / POST OFFICE BOX 2321
SANTA FE, NM 87504-2321 USA
(505) 988-4418

DEDICATION

For Nick

CONTENTS

Translator's Foreword ~ 9

Original Introduction ~ 11
1. Background ~ 15
2. Vicente Silva's Family ~ 18
3. Silva, Captain of Bandits ~ 20
4. The Assassination of Patricio Maes ~ 23
5. Silva's Escape and Emma's Capture ~ 28
6. The Assassination of Gabriel Sandoval ~ 31
7. Fruitless Search ~ 42
8. Robbery in Los Alamos ~ 45
9. The Disappearance of Telésfora Sandoval de Silva: ~ 47
Part 1 ~ 47
Part 2 ~ 50
Part 3 ~ 51
10. Justice Sleeps: ~ 53
Part 1 ~ 53
Part 2 ~ 56
Part 3 ~ 58
Part 4 ~ 58
11. Apprehension and Retribution of the Accomplices
in the Assassination of Gabriel Sandoval ~ 60
12. Assassination of Telésfora de Sandoval
and Retribution of Vicente Silva ~ 63

13. Distribution of Goods: ~ 68

Part 1 ~ 68

Part 2 ~ 69

14. Events Narrated by El Mellado: ~ 70

Part 1 ~ 70

Part 2 ~ 71

Part 3 ~ 72

15. Assassination of Benigno Martínez and Juan Gallegos ~ 73

16. Germán Maestas: His Marriage and Mishaps: ~ 75

Part 1 ~ 76

Part 2 ~ 77

Part 3 ~ 78

Part 4 ~ 78

17. Assassination of Tomás Martínez ~ 79

18. Gallardo Gives Notice of the Assassination: ~ 81

Part 1 ~ 82

Part 2 ~ 83

Part 3 ~ 83

19. The Thistle Camp ~ 85

20. The Honorable Lewis C. Fort ~ 86

21. Superior Judge Thomas Smith ~ 88

22. Conclusion ~ 92

Translator's Foreword

Vicente Silva, y Sus Cuarenta Bandidos, Sus Crímenes y Retribuciones (Vicente Silva and His Forty Bandits, His Crimes and Retributions) was originally written in Spanish and consists of twenty-one chapters describing in vivid detail the notorious and tragic events perpetrated by Vicente Silva and his bandits.

The chronicle was written by Manuel Cabeza de Baca, prominent citizen and lawyer of Las Vegas, New Mexico, during the time of Silva. He was my great grandfather. Las Vegas was a rowdy and lawless town in the late 19th century, generating notorious bad deeds and bad people. Manuel was outraged by the crimes inflicted on innocent people. The narrative was published by *La Voz del Pueblo*, a newspaper printing office in Las Vegas. My research brought to light another edition of the same book also published in 1896 by the Spanish American Printing Company.

The translation was begun by my aunt, Carmen Cabeza de Baca Pace, and on her death her children sent the unfinished manuscript to me. I translated the remaining chapters, including the Introduction and Conclusion, and added some biographical material on Manuel Cabeza de Baca.

Manuel Cabeza de Baca was educated at St. Michael's College in Santa Fe and at the Jesuit College in Las Vegas. He studied law and was admitted to the bar in 1880. In 1883 he was elected City Attorney of Las Vegas. He was elected to the House of Representatives for San Miguel County in 1886 and was chosen Speaker of the House. From 1889 until 1901 he served as State Superintendent of Public Instruction. It was he who found the body of Vicente Silva and claimed the three thousand pesos reward. The present narrative was written shortly after the body of Vicente Silva was found. Manuel died in 1915.

Manuel Cabeza de Baca was an actual eye-witness to the crimes committed by Silva and took an active part in the investigation of the bandits. This narrative provides a snapshot of frontier life and mores, thus giving a sociological insight into the lives of bandits and assassins in the West. The crimes committed included rustling, arson, rape, robbery and murder. At the time the narrative was written New Mexico was still part of the republic of Mexico. The lawless nature of Las Vegas at the time contributed significantly to the prevailing chaos and deterioration of law and order not only in New Mexico but in all of the Western states.

The manuscript used in this translation is available in only three libraries: Angélico Chávez Library, the University of New Mexico Library, and Baylor University Library. The English translation of the chronicle will make it available to a wider range of English-speaking readers.

In the preparation of this translation I am deeply indebted to the following people: my Aunt Carmen who recognized the historical importance of this document; my Pace cousins including Sharon, Howard, Richard, Don, Charles, and Linda who determined that the work my Aunt had begun not be lost; my husband, Nick Mills, who supported me and urged me on when I hit stumbling blocks; and my children, Nikos and Kyra, who repeatedly told me that I must continue on my quest.

I never knew my great grandfather, Manuel Cabeza de Baca; but on completing this translation I feel that I know him a bit better. I applaud his courage for giving us this snapshot into the town in which I grew up. Despite the many moves and destinations that have defined my life I will always consider Las Vegas my home.

—Dolores Gutiérrez Mills

Original Introduction

As I deliver this manuscript to the printer in which I narrate some of the most celebrated cases in the annals of criminality in New Mexico, it is not my intent to satisfy the most degenerate instincts of a certain class of readers who take pleasure in contemplating human misery in all its nakedness; nor is it my intent by publishing these pages covered in blood to satisfy the hunger of readers that gloat over scandalous chronicles.

No. My intention is totally a moral one. Although I depict human frailty in all its shortcomings and describe the bloodiest of crimes in the most vivid colors, my intention is not to scandalize but to portray the law breaker step-by-step on a journey that sooner or later leads to a jail cell. In a word, I wish to make it clear that behind every crime atonement for the crime inexorably follows. I also want to learn, and for my readers to learn, the tragic lessons that certain perverted individuals in our society have left us or—speaking more charitably—the lessons that certain defective and degenerate members of the human family have shown us.

Because in effect, the law breaker on committing a crime, often obeys the impulses of his free will and is aware of the crime committed; nevertheless, he is propelled to his actions by an unbalanced and imperfect brain and does not understand the severity of his actions. But whether the criminal is miserable and perverted or a sick person he infects society by his bad example and damages it by his heinous crimes and he should sacrifice himself at all costs in order to ensure society's peace and well-being. For this reason, the law sometimes deprives the criminal of his existence or prevents his contact with other men, and by imprisoning him behind the tall walls of the penitentiary, trusts that he will serve as an example to those inclined toward evil-doing and correct and cure the bad and diabolical habits of the criminal.

These passions and appetites of our miserable flesh, if they are not continually squelched by a profound and solidly-rooted religious sentiment, by fear of God, and by Christian morality, become the cause of the evil that man commits and are also the cause of the misfortune that daily bloodies men's hands. These crimes have caused many people to dress in mourning, have brought the ruin of families, have orphaned many young and innocent children, have spilled blood on scaffolds, and caused many fresh and promising lives to wither in the shadow of prisons. These crimes are also responsible for the ruin and decadence of many settlements that at one time flourished and were powerful. These crimes constantly invoke the just anger of the heavens and cause plagues and pestilence, floods, earthquakes, hunger and other calamities, and although these are entirely natural phenomena, they are, nevertheless, reminders from Providence that mankind has abandoned the path of virtue and justice.

If mankind strictly followed the saintly precepts of love and equity that The Ten Commandments embody, if we only lived by that sublime law of love and justice that was given to Moses on Mount Sinai in the midst of lightning and thunder, the world would be a paradise, men would truly be brothers, and human laws, tribunals and penitentiaries would not be needed. But man who is made of dust easily inclines himself toward slime and by committing sin stains the purity of the soul that is the spark of Divinity. Upon doing so, man exercises his free will and is completely aware of his actions, for God has given man free will to guide him along the path of life; man has absolute liberty to choose between good and evil. That is why God punishes man for not following His law, for He has given man that brilliant light of reason to guide him in the midst of the tempestuous passions of life. God also gives man the supernatural power of grace that helps him and protects him from the dangers of this world.

The evildoer has no excuses. Few are those who, because of anomalies in their makeup, embrace evil as something necessary to their human condition. Quite the contrary, all men aspire to moral perfection. Man instinctively raises his eyes to the heavens to contemplate the

Promised Land where in waves of celestial light he waits to free his soul from its bondage to his mortal body. Man instinctively loves goodness and gains satisfaction when he practices it. The practice of goodness is its own best reward. The satisfaction that the person who practices a good deed experiences is the voice of his conscience; it is the reward that God immediately sends to repay a meritorious action.

The voice of conscience, always strict and severe, makes its disapproval known in the soul of the person who deviates from goodness and with dark colors paints the evil action; man trembles, is horrified at himself, rejects evil and rectifies his evil ways. But again and again he fails and although he tries to correct his ways, little by little man's soul becomes perverted and corrupt with the habit of evil as man is deaf to the voice of his conscience until evil finally becomes his second nature. The evildoer seldom succumbs to his own impulses; he is usually helped by a partner in crime who seduces and perverts him. Bad companions are the cause of the perdition of many who—had they been left alone—would not have deviated from the straight and narrow path, but following the advice of bad companions, they go in search of their own destruction.

The evildoer, nevertheless, has no excuse, for the commission of all crime is contrary to natural sentiment. Furthermore, the penalty of law should keep him from committing crime, and if he tolerates the commission of crime by others, he should not tolerate it in himself, for the law punishes and threatens evildoers. The evildoer, however, is deaf to the voice of conscience, indifferent to God's law, and ignorant of legal penalties. He drinks the blood of his fellowman, steals his property and honor, and becomes a plague, a human beast, a rotten member of society. Once he reaches these heights the criminal does not retrace his steps; he cannot return to the bosom of the society that he has greatly offended and from whom he voluntarily separated himself. He faces the dangers of his situation with the cold calmness of the man who does not have God in his life and does not fear the dangers of life. But God is merciful and does not want the criminal's soul to be lost. Thus, He causes him to fall into the hands of human justice in order that a just punishment commensurate with the crime will be administered.

Such is the fortune of the hardened criminal who turns a deaf ear to the inspiration that heaven sends him but persists in his dangerous and fatal career and demonstrates the truth of the assertion of these pages in which we relate in clear language the truth of certain bloody episodes that bring shame to the community in which we live and are fresh in our memory. As stated initially, our purpose in relating this history is a moral one in which we wish to demonstrate how a group of bandits, after having mocked society for years, finally crumbled and one by one fell to pieces, already wounded by the vengeful ray of Divine cholera, and came humbly to receive their punishment on the altar of the august temple of human justice.

If we fulfilled our commitment, may it be for the greater good. If we failed, may our benevolent readers be indulgent with this inexperienced author that today brings to light his first product, without pretending to be a writer and trusting only in the kindness of the people of New Mexico.

—Manuel Cabeza de Baca

1
BACKGROUND

From time to time, God permits perverse monsters to materialize on the earth: cursed men who seem to have been spawned from hell itself, who leave a bloody trail on the pages of mankind. Some of these monsters possess, by some quirk of nature, "the face of an angel and the heart of a hyena," as is popularly stated.

Such a person was Joaquín Murrieta who, although peaceable in appearance, was abominable in deeds; a bandit, assassin and thief who for many years perpetrated his crimes in the state of California, killing in cold blood and stealing openly. Also in California another assassin named Durrant declared a war of extermination on young single women. In less than a month, Durrant killed Miss Lamont and Miss Minnie Williams in a church. He was given the maximum sentence for these crimes. Another assassin was Holmes from the city of Philadelphia who killed entire families and was a crafty thief. Because of his frightful crimes he has been labeled the "Champion of Assassins" in the annals of American Criminal Jurisprudence.

In addition, there was Diego Corrientes, a Spanish bandit, who assaulted people on the roadways and became famous for stealing from the rich to help the poor. History speaks to us of many other men, gifted by nature with a serene and tranquil appearance, who with their honeyed and persuasive tongues, declared a bloody war without mercy on their fellowmen. Many of their dreadful crimes, committed in cold blood, make us tremble in horror and indignation. These unspeakable crimes were committed for the mere pleasure of vengeance, greed, lust and pillage.

Vicente Silva, of sorrowful history, a man with an evil record, is the principal character in this true story. An account of some of his worst crimes and his sad and dreadful history provides us with enough subject matter to fill the pages of this book that I now offer to the public. A single narration of some of his unspeakable crimes and a portion of his sad and dreadful history and that of his accomplices make it unnecessary for this author to resort to a fictional analysis of the times.

Vicente Silva was born in the year 1845 in Bernalillo County, Territory of New Mexico. He grew up in a poor but respected family. He never attended school and consequently, was illiterate. His stature and strong physique gave him a more or less respectable appearance. He had a serious look about him, tempered by an expression of candor. Silva was pleasant and agreeable with everyone and because of this no one suspected that his appearance hid one of the most corrupt and evil souls in the world.

Everyone who knew Silva reports that it did not seem possible that such a man could have been born to rob and kill, carrying out his allegiance to Satan and harboring in his soul all the abominations, all the perversion, of which human misery is capable. Profound and depressing reflections come to mind when one recalls the history of such a human being transformed into a monster inciting destruction and giving free rein to his atrocities and bloodthirsty nature.

Vicente Silva resided in Las Vegas, New Mexico for more than fifteen years. Shortly after arriving in Las Vegas he opened a saloon and dedicated himself to the sale of liquor. Later he established a gambling hall on the same premises where the devotees of lady luck passed their time in dissipation and idle pleasure. By the years 1891 and 1892 he had many customers, particularly those that the law calls "vagrants" who never left the saloon. During all hours of the day and night Silva's saloon was filled with customers. Anything was possible there. The music with its harmonious tones attracted more and more idlers; drinks were freely distributed and toasts abounded. One could hear throughout the saloon the music of the revelers, the reproaches, the curses, and the imprecations from those already under the influence of searing liquor. The whole establishment was filled with singing, insults, and threats from drunken customers.

Men were not the only ones who occupied a prominent place in the saloon; there were also certain types of women present who were sponsored by the brotherhood and gave greater enthusiasm to its members. One of these women, known as "La Golondrina" (the Swallow) and two others known as "Las Elefantas" (the Elephants), were the nymphs of this Parnassus and the goddesses of Bacchus on whose altar they offered frequent libations.

The house where the protagonist of our story lived was two stories high. In addition to the saloon and gambling hall there were several rooms where Silva consulted with his accomplices. Silva was married and his family consisted of his wife, Doña Telésfora Sandoval de Silva, her brother, Gabriel Sandoval, and an adopted daughter whose origin and birth play a prominent part in this history.

2
Vicente Silva's Family

Doña Telésfora Sandoval de Silva, although not a beautiful woman, did not lack charm. She had a dark, clear complexion, and that alone makes a woman appealing. She had lovely dark eyes and long, silky lashes that still shone with the fire of youth tempered by the candor of honesty. She could not have been more than thirty years old. She adored her husband and dedicated herself to domestic tasks. She was not unaware that her husband possessed a soul stained by the filthy dust of crime, for Silva made no effort to hide his criminal acts from her. She admonished him and tried to give him good advice, but her advice—besides being ignored—cost her dearly when Silva responded with a slap, a curse, or an insult. She was a martyr who suffered in silence.

In the year 1885, a gentleman by the name of John Minner owned a livery stable where horses, carriages, and other kinds of vehicles and saddles were for hire. On the morning of March 5 of the same year Mr. Minner's stable hand went to feed the horses, as was his custom. Upon entering the manger he was surprised to discover a newborn baby girl in one of the stables. The stable hand told Mr. Minner of his discovery and the proper authorities were quickly informed. In a short time, everyone was talking about the baby girl that had been found in the stable but—although people conjectured and theorized about the discovery—no one could determine where the baby came from. The local authorities took charge and began looking for a charitable person who could care for the baby. Silva's wife, a humanitarian and a good Christian woman, convinced Silva to request that the authorities grant him custody. He honored her request, and the Prefect named Silva as guardian. Silva and his wife took the child to the baptismal font and she was given the name "Emma Silva."

As was to be expected, Mrs. Silva raised the child with as much care, patience and love as if she were her biological mother. Each day she loved the child more. Even Silva seemed to care for Emma and often took her to the saloon where the innocent child—like a violet lost in a mud puddle—was caressed by the filthy mob who frequented the establishment.

The child grew strong and healthy, and on her seventh birthday, she was sent to the Academy of Las Vegas. She was never late to school and progressed quickly in her studies for, if the truth be told, she was a dedicated student and was quite intelligent, which suggested good parentage. Her features and coloring and other indications, although indeterminate, pointed to Anglo-Saxon parents, although nothing positive was ever established.

Another member of the family was Silva's brother-in-law, Gabriel Sandoval, who was mentioned previously. Young Gabriel was about twenty years old and oversaw Silva's businesses, especially in his role as bartender. No one knew that Silva was perverse, and the Silva's were considered a happy family up until the time of the events that are recounted in this history.

3
SILVA, CAPTAIN OF BANDITS

In the year 1892 San Miguel County was genuinely concerned over the onset of widespread crime. The gang of bandits, with Vicente Silva as its captain, was committing all kinds of criminal offenses, and the garrison of police in charge of keeping the peace, establishing order, and demanding respect for the law were found, unfortunately, to be members of Silva's gang.

At nightfall, the people of Las Vegas were at the mercy of the assassins. People on the street were in grave danger of surrendering either their purse or their life into the hands of the gang and the night when no crimes were committed was rare. Fences were destroyed, the loss of hay and granaries was lamented; business establishments were burnt to the ground. The cries of a woman being violated were heard, and in the middle of the night hordes of men wearing face masks appeared. All in all, it was a horrifying and scary time.

Because these men were consummate hypocrites, they hid the infamy of their souls behind a sweet, inoffensive appearance; however, when they were assured of impunity, when it was time to act, they struck as the traitors they were. It seemed as if Silva and his gang was a family of demons escaped from hell with Divine permission.

Silva was enslaved to his business interests and his love of money; he had become greedy and quickly began to formulate plans to accumulate a fortune with minimal effort. In order to accomplish this, he organized a group of bandits that he named, according to the later confessions of his accomplices in crime, "The Society of Bandits of New Mexico" ("La Sociedad de Bandidos de Nuevo Mexico"). The following individuals were members of the Society: Julián Trujillo, José Chávez y Chávez, Eugenio Alarid, Martín Gonzales y Blea, alias "El Moro," Manuel Gonzales y Baca, alias "El Mellado," Guadalupe Caballero, alias "El Lechuza," Dionicio Sisneros, alias "El Candelas," Antonio José Valdez, alias "El Patas de Mico," Ricardo Romero, alias "El Romo," José F. Montoya, Florentino Medrán, Francisco Ulibarrí, Remigio Sandoval alias "El Gavilán," Néstor Herrera, Manuel Maldonado, Librado Polanco, Patricio Maes, Procopio Rael, Acacio Rael, Zenón Maes, Néstor Gallegos, Leandro Maestas, Germán Maestas, Hilario Mares, Marcos Varela, Gabriel Pitál, Genovevo Ávila, alias "El Cachumeno," Cecilio Lucero, Jesús Vialpando, Juan de Dios, Tomás and Sóstenes Lucero: the last three were members of the police force. Such were the men that comprised Silva's despicable army. The Society required that an oath of secrecy be taken by its members; thus, no one suspected that the brotherhood even existed.

The cattlemen of San Miguel, Mora, and Guadalupe Counties were suffering crippling losses of livestock and horses that mysteriously disappeared. No one knew who had stolen them or where they had been taken. Silva, on the sly, had purchased a ranch near the San Pedro mines known by the name of Monte Largo. Because of its natural and topographical setting the property was the ideal spot for the purpose that Silva had in mind. The aforementioned Ojo del Monte Largo (water spring of Monte Largo) situated in Santa Fe County, with its craggy ranges and practically impenetrable mountains, its deep canyons and inaccessibility, offered great advantages for sheltering the numerous animals that Silva herded there. This was the safest place for hiding the rustled animals and harvests stolen by Silva and his gang.

El Romo, the foreman in charge, kept watch over the interests of the Society from whom he received a salary. He also received a portion of the proceeds from the sale of beef that was sold to the miners in adjacent camps.

Silva maintained this clandestine operation for a long period of time without being noticed or discovered by anyone when, by a strange coincidence, a gentleman by the name of Refugio Esquibel learned that some of his lost horses were spotted with Silva's herd in Monte Largo. He immediately went to Silva's ranch and found his missing animals, some of which already bore the "V.S" brand. Mr. Esquibel took possession of his herd and drove them to Las Vegas where he confronted

Silva and demanded that he explain how he had acquired the horses. Silva was perplexed and unable to give a satisfactory explanation.

The Territory of New Mexico had recently been acquired by the United States and District Courts were in the process of being established. The threat that a Grand Jury might take notice of this and other more serious crimes in which Silva was personally involved convinced him that it was necessary to escape. Silva abandoned Las Vegas and the rumor was that he and some of his bandits were hiding out in El Coyote in Mora County which became his new center of operations. From this hideaway they continued inflicting their malicious misdeeds on the surrounding areas, committing all sorts of crimes without the slightest remorse. From that time on Silva was considered a bandit and a fugitive from justice.

Along with his criminal deeds, Silva abandoned his family who remained in Las Vegas from November 4, 1892, until a later time when they all mysteriously disappeared as our faithful readers will discover as events continue to unfold.

4

THE ASSASSINATION OF PATRICIO MAES

The night of October 22, 1892 was menacing and stormy. The peaceful citizens of Las Vegas took silent shelter in their respective homes, seeking rest and the nourishing warmth of their firesides. Because it was time for political campaigning the only ones out and about were the petty politicians who wandered from place to place and among markets seeking votes for county officials. At nightfall on that fateful day, it began to snow heavily and soon the earth was adorned with a white mantel. At that hour Silva's saloon had numerous customers; this included many criminals whose names were cited in the previous chapter.

Despite their excessive libation and their efforts to appear normal the faces of these individuals betrayed a certain prophetic and somber look. The bandits spoke to each other in whispers and some customers observed that they clandestinely slithered out to meet in a room nearby as if to consult with each other. Nevertheless, no one suspected that they were plotting something terrible, horrible, and wicked! As the clock struck twelve on that stormy night Silva surprised customers that were not members of the Society of Bandits of New Mexico by announcing that the saloon would close immediately as he was feeling indisposed. Very strange indeed, for Silva kept his establishment open twenty-four hours a day, every day of the year. Everyone left the saloon including the bandits who, one by one, went as far as Moreno Street and entered the saloon by a back door. Moreno Street had little or no traffic, especially at that hour of the night.

Once they were alone Silva and his cohorts who had gathered that night to discuss a grave matter formed a war council in order to judge one of their members that they considered guilty of the crime of treason. The council named as President Manuel Gonzales y Blea (El Mellado); Martín Gonzales y Blea (El Moro) was named secretary; Ricardo Romero (El Romo), and Remigio Sandoval (El Gavilán) were named marshalls; Silva was named prosecutor and Librado Polanco was appointed defender for the accused.

Patricio Maes, the accused, was present but was unaware of the purpose of this extraordinary meeting. He had come by special invitation and as one of Silva's favored employees, he obeyed the call and arrived promptly. The unfortunate man had no idea of the plot that would be leveled against him and he was caught like a fly in a spider web or like a rat who, while searching for food, falls into the trap.

Silva, acting as prosecutor, ordered that the accused stand before that diabolical tribunal and informed him that he was about to be punished by that satanical court for the crime of high treason. The defendant, despite being a member of the Society of Bandits and Robbers, was accused of informing Refugio Esquibel of the theft of his horses, thus placing all the members of the brotherhood in danger of being captured and punished by the law. And who did this unfortunate man think he was that he dared to incur the anger of the powerful Captain of the Bandits? None other than Patricio Maes, a member of the feared council, which wanted to be rid of him at all costs. Several charges were brought against Patricio Maes: in addition to the charge of treason, he was also accused of being on the brink of joining a law-and-order group called "The Society for Mutual Protection." This group was the most obstinate enemy of the bandits; it had been organized to help the legal authorities enforce the law and suppress crime.

The main charge presented by the prosecutor consisted of the following letter which was read aloud:

Rincón de La Tablazón, N.M.
October 7, 1892

Editor of El Sol de Mayo:
This is to inform you that on this day I am resigning from the Pueblo Unido Party because said Party, rather than helping the people and carrying out its promises, has imposed on them damaging laws.

Therefore, recognizing that the Republican Party is the true Party of the people, I align myself wholeheartedly with said Party and join the ranks of The Society for Mutual Protection.

(Signed) Patricio Maes

Patricio Maes vehemently proclaimed that he was innocent and promised to provide proof of his innocence if given sufficient time, but Silva and his bandits turned a deaf ear to his pleas. With unmerciful and unforgiving hearts, like monsters inured to committing the most horrible and despicable crimes in cold blood, they were insensitive to his entreaties, denied that he deserved clemency, and rejected his arguments without turning a hair. They wanted to add another victim to their Catalogue of Crime.

Manuel Gonzales y Baca (El Mellado) announced that the defendant's fate rested in the hands of the council. He said that Patricio Maes had committed an unpardonable crime, that he was a traitor and a liar, and that he must be held up as an example of the enforcement of the strictest punishment for his crime as a warning to the brotherhood and for their security and protection. Then, without further ceremony, the question of the life or death of Maes was put to a vote. The vote was divided: most of the bandits voted for clemency and recommended that a punishment less severe than death be imposed.

Of all the bandits El Mellado was the one most entrenched in crime; he seemed to thirst for human blood. Coolly and calmly, he chose not to announce the results of the vote but furiously threatened those who opposed the death sentence. He called them miserable cowards and other abusive names as befit his vocabulary. Polanco resented the insults and for a moment it seemed there might be a serious struggle. Polanco challenged El Mellado to a fight that would determine who would triumph in every place and under all circumstances. Silva and his other bandits, however, intervened and managed to calm the opponents. To avoid further controversy, Silva ordered three gallons of liquor and toasted everyone again and again until harmony was restored in that unlawful assembly of devils. Silva, El Moro, and El Mellado spoke in favor of punishing Maes with the death penalty, pointing to the risk that all the bandits ran in having so dangerous an enemy who could denounce them before the law. They concluded by asking the Council the following question:

"Who amongst you would like to go to the penitentiary?" "Nobody, nobody," they answered in unison. A second vote was taken, and the accused was unanimously declared guilty. He was sentenced to be hanged at the bridge of the Gallinas River.

El Gavilán immediately brought a rope that Silva had prepared previously. El Moro fashioned a loop that was placed on the unlucky man's neck who begged for pardon and mercy. The accused eyes seemed to be exploding as a torrent of tears burst from them! One can imagine the distress, the horrible pain that this wretched man experienced at finding himself face to face with the door to eternity. Before dying, Maes found himself surrounded by a hoard of unmerciful and barbaric executioners not worthy of the name of rational human beings! Hell itself would have shown more compassion toward that wretched man and would have been more sensitive to his pleas and lamentations, but those criminals—schooled in disgrace and crime and guided by their satanic star—remained unmoved as they proceeded to carry out their death sentence.

Silva ordered the bandits to put on their masks and march four by four toward the bridge. A rope was placed around Patricio Maes just as if he were an animal. Maes was terrified, but there was no hope; he was unable to scream, for El Gavilán and El Moro each held a gun to his head as they walked on either side of him.

The snow continued to fall, and the bandits took advantage of this. The group arrived at the bridge, which was three-hundred yards from the place where the condemned man would die. The streets were desolate and deserted. The residents of Las Vegas were enjoying the peace and tranquility of the evening, sleeping peacefully in their beds, and the footsteps of the bandits could not easily be heard. A sepulchral silence reigned. The darkness of the night was obscured by the tempest.

Patricio Maes, overwhelmed by the violence, bent down sadly as he walked. God only knows what thoughts went through the poor man's mind; what frenzied delirium trampled his afflicted heart. The only sounds heard from Maes were his frequent sighs, his plaintive moans, the pleas for mercy that agitated his beating and terrified heart! Now and again a weakly articulated word escaped from his lips, pleading for mercy, pardon and clemency in the name of Christ the Redeemer and Mary the Mother of the Forsaken; he uttered many other prayers and pleas capable of softening the hardest of hearts. The wicked bandits responded to his pleas with scornful laughter that stabbed at his tormented heart.

Upon arriving at the place of torture Patricio Maes, convinced that he would soon die, raised his eyes to heaven, uttered a prayer, and asked God to forgive him for having gone astray and sinned. He then surrendered his soul to the Creator.

The rope was tied to one of the iron beams of the bridge and the body of Patricio Maes was raised in the air by Silva and El Mellado, but the knot on the rope slipped and Patricio's unconscious body fell to the bottom of the river. Sisneros and El Gavilán descended into the river and grabbed the body while the others pulled on the rope until Patricio Maes was left hanging in the air.

The terrified bandits left, each going his own way. It continued to snow and soon there was not a single trace of their footsteps. The storm, in all its severity, seemed to favor the bandits. Early the next day Silva, in order to deflect suspicion from himself and spread another veil over the mysterious murder, sounded the alarm that the body of a man was hanging at the bridge.

Oh, if that bridge could have talked when the crowd gathered there to view the victim! If that bridge had been more than inanimate stone and iron it would have cried out to the hypocrite Silva: "You and your miserable bandits are responsible for this horrible assassination! You turned a deaf ear to his pleas and supplications! You are the scoundrel that tied the rope that hung him! You pushed him to his death! You are the treacherous villain assassin!"

The authorities lowered the body, identified it, and took it to the coroner where a postmortem was performed. A coroner's jury was appointed, and various witnesses testified, but despite the attempts that were made to shed some light on the assassination, nothing was determined conclusively. The entire affair remained wrapped in mystery and the bandits felt that they had escaped subsequent punishment.

5
SILVA'S ESCAPE AND EMMA'S CAPTURE

On November 7, 1892, the District Court convened its first session. Captain Esquibel filed a lawsuit against Silva charging him with the theft of his son's horses and other livestock that Silva hid in his Monte Largo ranch. The court issued a warrant for Silva's arrest, but because Silva was informed of this ahead of time, he took precautions to avoid being captured by the law, as a result of which the officials' efforts failed.

Doña Telésfora de Silva, Gabriel Sandoval, and Emma Sandoval remained behind in Las Vegas. For a short time, Mrs. Silva operated a restaurant in order to support her family. Young Emma dutifully continued her studies at the Academy. Although he had no reason for suspicion, Silva soon became jealous of his wife and brother-in-law. He feared they would inform the officials of his life of crime and reveal what they knew about the assassination of Patricio Maes. His family was aware of his terrible deeds but Silva, rather than trying to control his suspicions, allowed them to fester and fill his heart with sentiments of hatred and vengeance against his innocent family, sentiments that would later lead to his own perdition.

January 23, 1893 was a blustery day, one of the most intemperate of the season. The wind blew furiously. The frightful hurricane, which shook buildings, rose up wildly from the unfathomable void. It was a sad and mournful day, like all of the other days that Vicente Silva chose to transgress the law or engage in some other nefarious action. This monster, robed in human form, had a pact with the devil which supplied him with the most dismal days to commit his crimes.

On that day little Emma attended school as was her custom. About 10:00 a.m. a man appeared at the Academy and soon returned accompanied by Emma. He led her to a covered wagon that awaited at the gate. The two entered the wagon which departed at high speed in the direction of Los Alamos. Who would dare to remove a child from an educational institution in such a strange way?

Noontime came around and Mrs. Silva waited for Emma to come home, but she waited in vain for Emma did not appear. She became impatient at the child's tardiness, but the hours passed, and Emma did not come home. Could she have been kept after school? Mrs. Silva wondered. Emma never failed to come home at regular dinner hours.

Mrs. Silva, losing patience and tired of waiting, set out for the Academy in search of Emma. Upon arriving at the school, she inquired about Emma and to her surprise, some of the students told her that at ten o'clock Emma had entered a covered wagon with a man and disappeared. After Emma's disappearance Mrs. Silva was nearly out of her mind. Emma's absence caused her great sadness and her brain was feverish. She was like a mad woman walking the streets, going from house to house on that tempestuous day, asking everyone she met if they had seen Emma, whom she now considered her own child.

A few days passed and nothing was known with certainty about who had committed the kidnapping. After some time, investigations began to remove the veil placed over the incident and it was discovered that El Lechuza had taken Emma from the Academy and delivered her to Silva. This brought some consolation to Mrs. Silva for she assumed that Emma's life was not in danger; however, she was unaware of the motive of the unexpected kidnapping and never imagined that it was a prelude to her own death and that of her young brother. She still adored Vicente and never thought for a moment that he meant to do her harm, much less kill her.

A few days passed and Silva came home for the night and entered Mrs. Silva's bedroom. Acting the part of the hypocrite that he was and pretending great love for his wife, Silva begged her forgiveness for the scare she had suffered with Emma's disappearance. He said that the great love that he felt for Emma had been the motive for her kidnapping. Silva asked his wife not to be sad or impatient. He convinced her that he loved her as much as ever and that as soon as circumstances permitted, he would take her to see Emma. After praising his wife in this hypocritical manner, Silva quickly left her bedroom and returned to Los Alamos where he met with some of the gang members who had been waiting for him.

6
THE ASSASSINATION OF GABRIEL SANDOVAL

Silva was obsessed with the idea that he had to exterminate his wife. His malevolent, cruel and vicious instincts propelled him to this infamous act. A terrible impulse to assassinate had enveloped his heart. He could not stop thinking that his wife and young Sandoval, his brother-in-law, were planning to reveal his crimes to the authorities.

On February 12 Silva met in Los Alamos with El Mellado, Dionisio Sisneros, and El Lechuza to ask them to help him assassinate his wife and brother-in-law. At nightfall they hurried to Las Vegas, thirsting for human blood. The bandits approached Mrs. Silva's home from different directions and met at a previously agreed-upon location. When the bandits were all together, they sent El Lechuza to inspect the area which they called "The Enemy Camp."

El Lechuza was a shrewd character who knew how to carry out the orders entrusted to him. He snuck into Mrs. Silva's home. It was a dark night; not a star appeared in the sky. A thick black veil of clouds covered the heavens. It was bitterly cold. After speaking a few inanities to Mrs. Silva El Lechuza left the room pretending that nothing had happened. He met up with his cohorts and informed them that a lady and gentleman were visiting Mrs. Silva and her brother. On hearing this, Silva became completely undone and the only emotion that appeared on his face was the desire to kill. He proposed that the bandits storm the house and kill everyone, but El Mellado and Sisneros opposed the idea of making the visitors the victims of Silva's bloody furor. Silva had to agree with them even though it was against his will. The bandits decided to go their separate ways and reunite the following night at the same time and in the same place.

Dionisio Sisneros and El Mellado left for Los Alamos and Silva went straight to the home of his mistress, Flor de la Peña, who was the love his life and the repository of his secrets. Flor was not a beautiful woman, but she had a certain attraction that appealed to Silva's amorous ambitions. He had fallen in love with her, and she was the keeper of his heart. Flor was an exceptional woman; Silva could not have made a better choice to whom to reveal his secrets. Flor embodied the attributes that corresponded to her name: her stability and strength of character were rock-hard, and she had a masculine aspect about her.

Silva arrived at Flor's home which was situated at the edge of Las Vegas. There he found his beloved Flor alone in the house. Upon seeing Silva she ran to him saying, "Thank God you have come! This situation is unbearable; your wife is like a wild animal."

Silva responded: "What does it matter? Wild animals can be tamed, domesticated."

"There is no way to tame her," said Flor. "Her jealousy grows with each passing day. She has even threatened me and each night she watches my house."

Silva said, "Flor, I cannot live without you; that woman is standing in our way."

"Oh, my God!" exclaimed Flor, turning very pale. "What are you saying?"

"Nothing," Silva replied, "but what is in our way can easily be removed."

"I love you with all my heart, but what you imply is terrible," said Flor. "I don't understand, don Vicente."

The bandit repeated, "It is easy enough to understand; it is imperative that nothing should exist that might separate us, especially when that woman puts my life and liberty in jeopardy."

Flor looked anxiously at Silva and said, "I repeat, I do not understand you."

Silva said, "Sit down."

Flor sat down. Silva sat next to her, took her hands in his and said, "I love you with all my heart and I want you to be the repository of all my secrets. If all the crimes that you know I have committed and other crimes that necessity may oblige me to commit are not discovered, you shall be mine. Completely mine. You are my perdition and my salvation."

"Oh, what to do, what to do!" exclaimed Flor. "Your wife watches me constantly and if she is not watching me, it is her brother, Gabriel Sandoval watching. I am sure that one or the other of them has seen you enter my home this very night."

"Look," said Silva, pulling a dagger from his waistband. "Do you see this?"

"And what is that for?" asked Flor.

"With this dagger I shall finish off Telésfora and El Vejiga" (the bladder), which is what he called young Sandoval. "I must free myself of their tyranny and death is the surest way to quiet them."

"But that is horrible, don Vicente!" exclaimed Flor. "Don't you have a conscience? Killing your wife and your brother-in-law. What harm have they done you?"

"She is jealous," Silva answered, "and besides, I am afraid that they will reveal my crimes to the authorities, especially the assassination of Patricio Maes."

Flor said, "She has every reason to be jealous! She has every reason. You and I have not been discreet; we have given her numerous opportunities to discover that we are lovers, but that is not reason enough to take revenge in such a terrible manner. I do not think she will denounce you to the authorities. She is a good person who loves you very much, and she would not do such a thing. And I don't think Gabriel is worth worrying about. His only concern is Emma's disappearance and if you return her to them, I believe they will be happy and leave you in peace."

"It is impossible to avoid this," said Silva. "That woman is extremely jealous: she follows you, spies on you, and questions everyone about our affair."

"But is there no other way, don Vicente?" asked Flor.

"There is not," said Silva. "The electric spark is faster than a locomotive. She has been seen speaking to my worst enemies; if that woman betrays me, and if El Vejija testifies against me, I am doomed. The dead have no recourse to a tribunal; we would be in peace with nothing to worry about."

"Nothing to worry about?" Flor screamed. "If you kill your wife and Gabriel, don't you think the authorities would come looking for you?"

"No," said Silva, "Because no one would know. I will perform the act in such a secret way that the victims will disappear, and nobody will know if they are alive or dead, or where they are."

"My God!" screamed Flor.

"And it will be useless for them to suspect me for not a trace of them will be left; people will say that Telésfora and Gabriel have gone with me, that they are with me."

"No, never!" exclaimed Flor, for although she was passionately in love with Silva, she had not thought that she would have to consent to the crime he was proposing.

"No," Silva said in a hoarse and somber voice, "I will make them disappear and you and I will hide away in Mexico or in some country in South America, and no one will know where we are. I need you to be completely mine. You know I have sufficient means and friends to get safely away."

"Have pity, don Vicente!" cried Flor. "Think of our unborn child, the fruit of our passion."

"You either love me or you don't. If you love me, you will agree with everything I propose, be quiet, and follow me. If you don't love me, well, we shall see..." Silva exclaimed with a terrible and menacing expression as he walked to the table where he picked up his hat as if preparing to leave.

"Wait!" exclaimed Flor, rushing suddenly toward Silva. "Are you abandoning me?"

"Yes," replied Silva, "but I am leaving with the intention of finishing off this cursed family."

"This is terrible," cried Flor. "If only there were some other way."

"There is no other way. This must happen as I say, sooner or later. That woman and that young man are in my way and I hate them. Their lives weigh on me and I must remove myself from this critical situation at all costs," said Silva.

"And what will you do?" asked Flor anxiously.

"What will I do? I will look for Gabriel and Telésfora and when the time is right I will do away with them. I have plans to take care of Gabriel this very night and I will take care of Telésfora later," Silva said.

"I am afraid, don Vicente," Flor cried, "what you plan to do is terrible, exceedingly cruel."

"Let's end this," said Silva. "You must agree with our plans, so be quiet. More than likely by tomorrow night it will all be over, or at least partially over."

Flor finally complied and said no more.

The following day Silva was hiding in Flor's house. Three policemen—José Chávez y Chávez, Julián Trujillo, and Eugenio Alarid, who were members of Silva's gang, came to visit Silva. They formulated new plans and Julián Trujillo, a man of good standing in the community who had an intelligent and kind look about him and was above suspicion, took charge of watching young Sandoval's every step. Trujillo was Gabriel's closest friend and could betray him in the most vicious manner without young Sandoval being aware of this treachery.

As mentioned previously, Silva had kidnapped Emma. This provoked such anger in young Sandoval that he decided to find out where Emma was being held and upon discovering that Silva had her, he had taken to watching Flor's house trying to find out if the child was there.

On February 13, young Sandoval met Julián Trujillo in front of Silva's Imperial Saloon. As was his custom, he greeted him and the following dialogue took place: "How are you, my friend, Julián?"

Trujillo answered, "I am well, Gabrielito. And how are you?"

"Like the devil," answered Gabriel. "You know that Silva has kidnapped Emma, and I wish that the devils would take him to hell for being a thief."

"So I have heard," said Julián, "but you know that I am your friend and if you are interested in finding Emma, tonight might be the best time to do that. I have heard through the grapevine that Silva will be at Flor's house tonight and that he will have Emma with him."

"I appreciate your telling me this, dear friend. You know that my sister, Telésfora, is sick with worry since Emma's kidnapping and she would gladly give up half her life to see her again. If, as you say, old man Vicente will be at Flor's house tonight, you can be sure that my sister and I will be spying on him and we will notify the sheriff so he can rescue the child."

"I will be happy to help you out tonight. You know that I am your friend and you can depend on me," said Julián, "but an idea just occurred to me that should make Emma's rescue from the hands of Silva a success. As you know, I myself, José Chávez y Chávez and Eugenio Alarid are policemen and we can take charge of spying on Flor's house.

You can join us if you like. If we find Silva we will apprehend him and take him to jail."

Gabriel said, "Good thinking, my friend, Julián. I will accompany you on your search and, God willing, the old villain will finally fall into the hands of the law."

"Well, get ready to join us. Tonight at eight o'clock we will wait for you at the Imperial Saloon, but meanwhile I advise you not to say a word of this to anyone if our plan is to work. Do not breathe a word of this plan even to your sister, Telésfora. Her joy will be much greater if we surprise her by bringing Emma to her when she least expects it."

"Agreed," said young Sandoval, and since it was almost six o'clock he took his leave from Julián, but not before shaking his hand and expressing his gratitude for Julián Trujillo's frank and sincere manner and for the help he had so willingly given him.

A man who was standing close to Gabriel and Julián was listening to everything they said and remembered all that had transpired between them, word for word. This was Guadalupe Caballero, previously referred to in our story as El Lechuza. El Lechuza's short stature, crossed eyes, long hair, and dirty face contributed to his melancholy appearance; however, nothing in his expression or physiognomy suggested that he was a wicked man or someone capable of hurting another human being. He was one of those people upon whom nature has placed a mask so that others are unable to discern the perversity of his soul. El Lechuza was generally found sitting in the sun during the winter months and in the most conspicuous places in the summer. His usual posture was to sit on his haunches with his elbows on his knees and his cheeks resting in the palms of his hands. He appeared to be tame as a lamb or a beggar in his torn and dirty clothes; he seemed unable to carry on an intelligent conversation and his movements were stumbling, but all of this was a cover-up for what El Lechuza was in reality.

Underneath that humble appearance, beneath those tattered clothes, El Lechuza harbored a violent character, a stone-cold heart, a soul without pity, and a limitless ability to plunder. At night fall, El Lechuza was not the person thus far described: at that time, he mounted his horse, rode like the wind, and circling the cattlemen's haciendas, seized the fattest cattle. Before sun up, as a result of his nocturnal mission, he sold the stolen cattle to meat markets with which he had previously made secret arrangements. El Lechuza was Silva's right-hand man. He was the one who successfully transported the stolen cattle to Monte Largo. He was Silva's most trusted ally and his spy in all his transactions.

As mentioned previously, El Lechuza had eavesdropped on the conversation that had taken place between young Sandoval and Trujillo outside of the Imperial Saloon. As Sandoval took leave from Trujillo he looked over his shoulder and upon spotting El Lechuza he became enraged and walked toward him. Sandoval knew that El Lechuza was Silva's confidante, that it was he who had taken Emma from the Academy and led her into the wagon that caused her to disappear. Sandoval directed a few insults at El Lechuza, calling him a miserable thief and other disgraceful names, but El Lechuza—who was a diplomatic villain— offered numerous excuses saying that he had not had anything to do with Emma's kidnapping, that he liked Telésfora more than he did Silva, and that he was prepared to assist in Emma's rescue. Young Sandoval was about to slap El Lechuza but Trujillo intervened and without ceremony and full of anger, Sandoval set out for sister's house.

El Lechuza turned and headed toward National Avenue, walked down a few intersections, and set out for Flor de la Peña's house where Silva was staying. He entered Flor's house and told Silva everything that had transpired between Trujillo and young Sandoval and lastly, between himself and Sandoval. Silva recognized that Trujillo had done his job well, that he had laid out the preliminary steps and had devised a plan that Silva agreed with. The plan for the assassination of young Sandoval so pleased Silva that he approved of everything that had been agreed upon between Trujillo and young Sandoval. He ordered El Lechuza to follow young Sandoval and to ask the rogue policemen Julián Trujillo, Chávez y Chávez and Eugenio Alarid to meet him in a hidden alley situated in front of the old Gonzales mill some distance from town. The dark, narrow alley was perfect because no one dared venture there after night fell. Silva and the aforementioned "policemen" would meet there at eight o'clock in order to consult and finalize their plans. El Lechuza did as Silva ordered him without wasting any time. He returned to the plaza and hid in order to observe each step and every movement of young Sandoval.

Silva arrived punctually at the meeting place a few minutes before the agreed-upon time and did not have to wait long before the "policemen" joined him. These three men had sworn to keep the lives and the property of the people of San Miguel County safe. As guardians of the public peace, they had sworn to uphold the law and were obligated to act in the interests of the community but rather than upholding their sacred trust to uphold the law, these men were conspiring with a vile bandit, the worst enemy of society, and planning to assassinate a young man who had never harmed them, a young man who was only now beginning to enjoy the fruits of life. This gullible young man considered the "policemen" his friends and never imagined that the paid protectors of the county government might be capable of harboring evil thoughts in their hearts, much less attempt to kill him.

Silva praised the "policemen" for their punctuality and assured them that they would be well paid if they helped him to execute his plans. He wanted them to trick young Sandoval into accompanying them to a secluded spot where Silva could drive the dagger into Sandoval's heart without anyone being aware of his actions. Julián Trujillo started to give Silva an account of the events that had transpired in the vicinity of the Imperial Saloon but because Silva had heard the whole story from El Lechuza, he interrupted Trujillo saying there was no time to be lost in idle conversation. Silva was enraged; the idea of cold-blooded murder had taken over his brain, and he wanted to carry out his plans and to carry them out with impunity.

Everything was decided in a few words. The "policemen" were instructed to find young Sandoval and bring him with them to Flor's house. Silva suggested that they take young Sandoval down the alley that connects with the Catholic Cemetery and from there to continue by the abandoned ruins of the old Mayor's house (as it was known) that was now in ruins with only the walls left standing.

José Chávez y Chávez, Alarid and Trujillo left that mournful place; their footprints were the only trace left of those who would soon become the assassins of young Sandoval. People that pass by that place now say, "This is where Silva and his "policemen" confirmed their plans to assassinate young Sandoval. This is where the "policemen" Chávez, Trujillo and Alarid violated their oath of office when they delivered themselves to the inhuman designs and strategies of Vicente Silva." The guardians of peace returned to the plaza from all different directions in search of the lamb who soon would be sacrificed for the sake of vengeance and who would die beneath the dagger of the aggressive and ferocious Silva.

Meanwhile, Gabriel Sandoval was filled with confidence that with the help of the police Emma would be rescued that night. As we said previously, Gabriel, upon taking his leave of Trujillo in front of the Imperial Saloon, went directly to his sister's house. He was happy as a lark at the thought of giving her the good news and the most promising hopes possessed him. He was certain that Emma would be rescued that night. This is what Gabriel wanted most of all; he did not care if Silva was arrested or not. He hastened to arrive quickly at Telésfora's house and, filled with enthusiasm, he burst into her bedroom. Gabriel was crazy with happiness as he told his sister the wonderful news.

Telésfora could not help but be filled with happiness. Like young Sandoval she believed that their greatest hopes and dreams were about to be realized. Sandoval told his sister everything that had transpired just as he remembered it, without leaving anything out. He even told her that Trujillo had admonished him not to breathe a word of their plans to anyone, not even to her, but Telésfora was extremely anxious and nervous and her only desire was to see Emma. She begged Gabriel to allow her to accompany him to Flor's house to rescue Emma, but he made her see that this was not the prudent thing to do for the situation was too delicate and dangerous. After arguing for some time Telésfora finally agreed to let young Sandoval handle all the details concerning Emma's rescue.

At approximately eight o'clock that same night Gabriel left his sister's house ready to pursue his inquiry and make a fool of Silva. The young man met with the "policemen" outside the Buffalo Saloon at about 9:30 that night. They continued down the street that runs in front of the Catholic Church and went in the direction of Flor's house. They went through the alley suggested by Silva, turning in the direction of the old Mayor's house. As they approached the solitary and demolished house, Silva, quick as a flash, jumped out of his hiding place and, while Chávez and Alarid held Sandoval's arms, that beast who enjoyed human suffering and who had listened to Patricio Maes's humble supplications for mercy, trembling in the presence of death, remained implacable to Sandoval's pleas. Silva was about to sink the dagger into young Sandoval's heart in the presence of those who wore the insignia of peace pinned to their chests, in the presence of those who should have protected him. Sandoval, upon seeing the dagger in his brother-in-law's hand, immediately understood that he had been lied to, betrayed, that the "policemen" were paid assassins, and that he would soon die! But why? He could not imagine why! Sandoval instinctively fought to free himself from those ferocious brutes, but they held his arms tight. He could do nothing to defend himself. This was the most unlucky and terrible night of his life.

"Now I must make you understand, young man, that your plans and those of your sister will not come to fruition," Silva growled with his accustomed roar, like that of a lion.

"I don't know what plans you are referring to, brother Vicente," the young man who could barely speak answered.

"I am referring to the scheme that you are planning against me; that you want to ruin me and that you want to reveal everything you know about me," said Silva.

"By the holy name of God, that is not true! Neither my sister nor I have even thought about doing anything like that."

"You lie!" answered the archangel of darkness, and he aimed his dagger at Sandoval in order to stab him.

The young man made one more attempt to free himself from those traitors of the law, but he was unable to do so. He slumped to his knees at Silva's feet and pleaded with a voice that the terror he felt made almost unintelligible, "Mercy! Mercy, brother! Have mercy on me for I have never done anything to offend you!"

"Die, you wretched traitor, die!" said Silva, and immediately Chávez and Alarid discharged their guns into the head of the defenseless youth, while Silva plunged his dagger into Sandoval's chest. Sandoval's lifeless body dropped to the ground and the bandits carried it into the abandoned house. Silva gave Eugenio Alarid some money and ordered him to act as a sentinel at the intersection of Moreno and South Pacific Streets. He instructed Chávez and Trujillo to wait for him behind Flor's house and he took off in the direction of El Lechuza's house. El Lechuza was aware of the entire situation and he waited patiently for Silva to appear. He had a horse ready for any emergency.

"Hello, Guadalupe! Is the horse I ordered ready?"

"Just as you ordered," answered El Lechuza, and added, "And how are things going?"

"Like wind on the stern. The deed is done. I have just dispatched El Vegija," (his nickname for young Sandoval). "Take your horse and follow me." El Lechuza followed his master's command and did as he was asked.

Both men went in the direction of the ruins where young Sandoval's body lay. "Here is the body of the man who insulted you not so long ago!" said Silva pointing to Sandoval's body that lay in a pool of blood. "Tell him to insult you now," he added sarcastically. After staring at his innocent victim for a few minutes Silva said, "Ah! The old-timers were right when they said that vengeance is sweet; that vengeance is the preferred delicacy of the gods."

The two men stepped out and headed in the direction of Flor's house where Chávez and Trujillo awaited them. While they were discussing the best way to hide the cadaver Silva sent El Lechuza for a bottle of whiskey. It was not long before he returned because, as his nickname suggested, El Lechuza was a nocturnal bird of prey whose vision was better by night than by day.

In the spirit of the god Bacchus, the bandits celebrated their shameful deed. They toasted each other, amongst them the sweet Dulcinea; they toasted to the health of "The Captain of the Bandits of New Mexico." On concluding the toasts the four men headed to the sacrificial spot. Silva and El Lechuza lifted Sandoval's body by the arms, while Julián Trujillo held the legs. They carried him down the street until they arrived at a run-down house on Moreno Street, almost facing the building that housed Silva's saloon. Chávez followed the funeral cortege holding the horse's bridle. Upon arriving at the aforementioned place, they tossed Sandoval's body into a pit that in the past had served the miserable assassin as a latrine, and covered the hole with dirt and trash. The deed was done. Young Sandoval disappeared mysteriously leaving not a single trace.

7
FRUITLESS SEARCH

Mrs. Silva had not slept a wink all night. She had been unable to sleep as she waited impatiently for her brother's return. She was filled with dread and imagined each noise she heard to be the arrival of her brother and little Emma. That night seemed endless for the poor woman. The next day, Mrs. Silva, impatient and anxious to discover what had happened to her brother, took off and went to consult with the author of this account, Manuel Cabeza de Baca. She told him of the sudden and unexpected disappearance of her brother. Feeling compassion for Mrs. Silva and believing that this was a grave matter, for nothing less could be expected from Silva and his accomplices, Mr. C. de Baca promised Mrs. Silva that he would make the necessary investigations. Somewhat consoled, Mrs. Silva left with the hope that the proper investigations would begin immediately.

It was approximately six p.m. on February 14, the day after young Gabriel's disappearance, when the author of this story went to the office of the Justice of the Peace who at this time was José L. Galindre, a fair and honest man. He knocked at the door and was invited to enter. Mr. Galindre was alone in the office.

The judge said, "Hello, Mr. Baca, what has occurred that I have the pleasure of seeing you here?"

"The law should be sought when it is needed."

"So tell me...," the judge replied.

"Well, I need the Police Chief to look for a young man who has gone missing."

"Deuce! That sounds serious! Sometimes we are asked to look for young women that are missing, but men..."

"The loss of a young man is always more serious than the loss of a woman."

"Do I detect a bit of egotism in that remark?" replied the judge smiling.

"Let me explain. A woman might be missing because her lover takes her away, and while her family suffers greatly, the woman is quite happy. When a man goes missing and cannot be found, he might easily be in a hospital or on the brink of a suicide attempt, or..."

"And do you fear that something like that has happened to the young man you seek?"

"I am afraid so, since about nine o'clock last night Gabriel Sandoval has not been seen despite the fact that his sister and friends have looked everywhere for him. I must explain to you that young Sandoval, were he alive, would not fail to go to his sister Telésfora's home at mealtime and to sleep, because he is like that, always very punctual. Consequently, I fear some harm has befallen him."

The judge stepped out of his office and returned in a few minutes saying he had left word for the Chief of Police to join them. The latter, in effect, appeared a few moments later.

"Mr. Galindre," the Chief of Police said, "What can I do for you?"

"Mr. Baca would like to know the whereabouts of Gabriel Sandoval who has gone missing. We want you to conduct a full-scale investigation and to marshal all of your resources in this effort."

"The entire police force has already been advised of that matter," the Chief of Police said. "I have already been notified of that young man's disappearance. I have conducted some initial investigations but have not been able to find him; I believe it is entirely possible that he has left town."

"Considering his condition and his habits," observed Mr. C. de Baca, "Gabriel would have said goodbye to his sister before leaving town for he is an obedient and loving brother. That is why I suspect he has met with some misfortune."

"In any case," said the judge to the Police Chief, "it is necessary that you send out all your greyhounds to investigate the whereabouts of young Sandoval."

"I will do that immediately and do everything possible so that no more time is lost in finding that young man," the Police Chief said.

The Police Chief left the judge's office and headed toward police headquarters. Once there, he summoned Trujillo, Chávez, and Alarid and informed them of the matter at hand. They promised they would leave no stone unturned until they located the young man. They pretended to look, but of course, they never came close to the latrine where they themselves had buried Gabriel's body. Their final report indicated that they could not find a single clue connected to the missing person; however, they had heard a rumor that a man was found hanging from a pine tree at Kearney's Gap and this might possibly be the person they were looking for.

Mrs. Silva knew that Julián Trujillo had persuaded Gabriel to accompany him in the entrapment of Silva and the rescue of Emma; she decided to visit Trujillo regarding the mysterious disappearance, but it was all in vain. Trujillo denied everything, protesting that he had not seen Gabriel on that unlucky night. He even pretended to be hearing of the disappearance for the first time, and offered to join Mrs. Silva in her search for Gabriel. He took Mrs. Silva to Kearney's Gap in a carriage where they looked all around the mountain and the surrounding area but could find nothing. They returned to town satisfied that the story of the hanging man was only a rumor. The case of the missing Gabriel remained an impenetrable mystery.

8
ROBBERY IN LOS ALAMOS

The interminable rain that fell on the night of April 6, 1893 might well be compared to that of the Great Flood. The violent action of the strong wind formed clouds so thick that it was difficult to distinguish objects at any distance. Occasionally, the vivid flash of lightning quickly lit up the sky, this was followed by an explosive clash of thunder that made the earth tremble. That gloomy night was chosen by the subject of this history to commit another of his heinous crimes.

A gentleman by the name of William Frank operated a trading post in the community of Los Alamos. The store was stocked with all the commodities and provisions necessary for the ranchers in the community. A number of homes had been built along the Sapello River; the occupants of these homes dedicated themselves to farming and were regular customers of Mr. Frank's store. This obliged Mr. Frank to keep his store well stocked with food and other provisions that the farmers might request. The store was situated some distance from the farmers' homes; the closest house was where Mr. Frank lived, approximately three hundred yards distant from his store.

When Silva decided to rob Mr. Frank's store, he called a meeting with El Mellado, El Moro, El Patas de Mico, and Dionicio Sisneros y Medrán in order to discuss his latest project with them. They all agreed to the plan, for they were convinced that Mr. Frank's safe was filled with cash. They decided to send Medrán to buy a quart of liquor at the store, and Silva gave him a twenty dollar gold piece for this purchase. Medrán was instructed to follow Mr. Frank when he went to get change for the gold piece and to try to estimate how much money was in the safe. Medrán left on his mission and returned quickly for the store was not more than six hundred yards from the bandits' hiding place.

Mr. Frank had no reason to suspect his customers and did not hesitate to open his safe in order to make change for the gold piece. Medrán followed him and stopped at a distance which allowed him to observe how much money was in the safe. It appeared to the bandit that there was no less than three hundred pesos in the safe, and he reported this to his Captain.

Silva and his companions waited anxiously for nightfall but they became impatient when the clock struck eleven p.m., the agreed-upon time for their adventure to begin. Then, donning their face masks, they went in the direction of Mr. Frank's store. They broke in the main entrance, lit some lamps, and began their nocturnal task. The safe weighed at least a ton and after numerous unsuccessful efforts they finally decided to use levers to pull it. They then placed the safe in the carriage they had brought for that purpose. This task being accomplished, they transported the safe to a hidden place on the outskirts of town, unloaded it from the carriage, and immediately returned to the store where they reloaded the carriage with all kinds of food and merchandise. They took as much as Silva's horse and the bandits could carry.

The following morning a good part of Mr. Frank's merchandise was at El Coyote, which was one of Silva's hideouts. The bandits broke open the safe, but to their disappointment found only forty pesos, numerous postage stamps, and a number of promissory notes. The darkness of the night had worked in their favor as it had on other occasions, and it seemed like the Angel of Darkness had protected them. It had provided the fearsome elements to cover-up their crime and where Silva and his gang set foot, no trace was left behind.

Silva and his cohorts were not content with simply looting the Frank store, but attempted to follow the example of the celebrated Spanish bandit, Diego Corrientes. In doing what they saw as a great favor to Mr. Frank's debtors, they set fire to account books, cash books, and all papers necessary for Mr. Frank to collect on debts owed to him. Mr. Frank lost 10,000 pesos that night.

Silva, satisfied with his work and convinced that his deeds had greatly benefited the community, gave thanks for the storm that had favored them, left the village and headed for the comfort of the den of thieves.

9

THE DISAPPEARANCE OF TELÉSFORA SANDOVAL DE SILVA

PART 1

As might be expected after the recent events, Mrs. Silva was grieving and deeply sad. Emma's kidnapping and the disappearance of her young brother, Gabriel, caused her great suffering and she did not know what to think. One day, as she reflected deeply on the sorrow that overwhelmed her, she heard a knock at the door. "Who could that be?" she asked herself. She was fearful, but a second knock caused her to inquire who was there.

"It is I," said a voice that was none other than El Lechuza's, "I have a letter for you from Gabriel Sandoval."

Mrs. Silva no sooner heard that name than she hastened to answer the door. Filled with joy and impatient to receive any notice on the whereabouts of her brother, she asked, "What did you say? Where is Gabriel?"

El Lechuza showed her the letter and said, "This letter will tell you everything. Goodbye." And placing the letter in Mrs. Silva's hand, El Lechuza disappeared as quickly as lightning.

Mrs. Silva was astonished and could not explain to herself El Lechuza's sudden appearance. Her hand trembled and she considered tearing up the envelope out of fear of being disillusioned by its contents. She thought she might find some mystery or sad and disagreeable news in the letter. After some trepidation, she finally decided to read it. Closing the door, she approached the lamp, and with a trembling hand she tore open the envelope and glanced at the signature which read, "Gabriel Sandoval." At that moment her heart throbbed with happiness for it was filled with joy and relief at what she believed was a letter from her brother which told her that he was alive, safe, and out of danger. She began to read the letter which said the following:

El Coyote, New Mexico
18 April 1893

Mrs. Telésfora Sandoval de Silva
Las Vegas, New Mexico

My esteemed and never forgotten sister who has all my love and affection:

I do not doubt for one moment that since my disappearance from Las Vegas you have had a sad and trying time because you did not know my whereabouts. Fortunately, I can take this opportunity to allay all your fears. Dearest sister, I am exceedingly sorry that I caused you so much pain because of my sudden and unexpected departure from Las Vegas which was due to circumstances of which you are well aware.

That night when I was on my way to meet the policemen who were to help me rescue Emma, I unexpectedly ran into Vicente before meeting up with the policemen. He treated me in a kind and loving way such as he had never done before. He explained the situation to me and begged me to accompany him to El Coyote to take charge of his smuggled interests there. I accepted his offer and came to El Coyote. I meant to inform you sooner about what is happening here but until this moment, I had not had the pleasure of doing so because we are in a deserted and desolate place with few means of communication with the outside world.

My brother, Vicente, has treated me like a prince, better than if I were his own son. All that is lacking is that you should come and join us. Emma is well and very happy. Don Antonio and his family are extremely hospitable and enjoy having us as their guests. We sit around in the evenings listening to my brother and his companions tell stories about their adventures and mishaps. We now have a wagon and a buggy and a good supply of groceries. We also have a large number of the finest horses.

Brother Vicente is thinking of going to Las Vegas to bring you here. I hope you will consider coming so that you may benefit from the comforts which we enjoy. If my brother, Vicente, is unable to go to Las Vegas, he will send El Cachumeno, who is a faithful and trustworthy man, to bring you to Los Alamos. With the person that picks up your furniture my brother, Vicente, will notify you what day I can expect you to be in Los Alamos for he wants you to be with us and I feel confident that you will be.

My brother, Vicente, has had great success in all his enterprises. He takes great risks and I expect that one of these days he will arrive here with the entire warehouse of Browne & Manzanares. He is capable of doing this.

Emma sends her love and I, your affectionate brother, anxiously await your arrival.

(Signed) Gabriel Sandoval
p.s. Sister, when you come, please bring the dogs. We miss them.

As Mrs. Silva read and reread the letter all her worries and suspicions vanished. She believed the letter was genuine and she was filled with happiness. Tears rolled down her cheeks and she decided to forget all the hurt and pain Silva had caused her. She was determined to hurry to his side where she believed she would find young Sandoval and the child, Emma. She never imagined that this might be a trap set by Silva to send her to her grave. Mrs. Silva surrendered herself to serious reflection. Thousands of ideas crossed her tormented mind.

I will go to him and advise him to stay away from evil, she thought. If today his confused mind, his corrupt heart is unable to distinguish good from evil, some day he will recognize the error of his ways and implore God to forgive his crimes. Don Vicente is good to me and who better than I who know him so well, who love him so much, to bring him back to a life of virtue. I will do so with my tears and with my prayers. Mrs. Silva wept abundantly, for she had a tender and sentimental heart. It was her destiny to suffer and to weep. She was prepared to follow her husband, prepared to undergo whatever martyrdom might be necessary in order for her to do that. Her entire life had been an eternal suffering.

Silva was a cruel despot. For Mrs. Silva her marriage had been a Calvary. Fifteen years ago a priest had united them at the foot of the altar and since that time not a single complaint had left her lips. Silva's indifference, his bad conduct, his cruelty toward her, had done nothing to extinguish the pure love that she felt in her heart for him. She accepted her hardships with calmness and resignation. That is how things stood. In the end, her husband's aberrations had made him a fugitive from justice. Mrs. Silva passed her days in solitude and abandonment until the occurrence of the events that I will now recount.

PART 2

On May 19th, when the light of day was just beginning to scatter the shadows of the night, Florentino Medrán arrived at the home of Mrs. Silva in a wagon pulled by a pair of horses. Mrs. Silva had just gotten up and was busy starting a fire in the fireplace in order to prepare her breakfast. She knew Medrán well and when he called at the door she recognized him and let him in. After the usual greetings, Medrán handed Mrs. Silva a letter. She tore open the envelope and read as follows:

Los Alamos, New Mexico
18 May 1893

My dear Doña Telésfora,

I hope that the receipt of this letter finds you enjoying good health. Gabriel, Emma and I are well, thanks to God. Florentino Medrán has a carriage that will bring your furniture and your other belongings to El Coyote where we will establish a temporary residence.

I trust that you will send your furnishings with Medrán today. Tonight, after dark, Genovevo Avila will pick you up and bring you here. I will be waiting for you at Cañada Pastosa, and upon your arrival, I will send you on to meet with Gabriel and the child.

Keep your departure from Las Vegas as secret as you can.

With no more for now, receive the heart of your husband who would much rather see you in person than write to you.

(Signed) Vicente Silva

It did not take Mrs. Silva long to prepare for her departure and, since she did not have much to transport, in less than two hours Medrán was on his way back to Los Alamos. Mrs. Silva wrote her husband a few lines to advise him that she would leave with El Cachumeno on that very evening as he had suggested.

El Cachumeno, who appeared to be an honorable man, but was in reality like a bad omen, arrived punctually at Mrs. Silva's house in a buggy as the sun was setting. Mrs. Silva mounted the buggy and they hurried to Los Alamos. They followed the least traveled route. Silva and El Lechuza were waiting for them at Cañada Pastosa which is about halfway between Los Alamos and Las Vegas.

Part 3

When Silva left Los Alamos to meet his wife, five of his bandits remained behind awaiting their return. As might be expected of people of this caliber, while they waited they were possessed of only one thought: Silva's selfishness. He incited them to commit all sorts of crimes without rewarding them sufficiently. The bandits knew that Silva carried a considerable sum of money with him; by their calculations, this sum was no less than nine thousand pesos. Overcome by greed, they mutually decided to take possession of Silva's fortune at the first opportunity, and decided there was no time better than the present to accomplish this. Silva's fortune was within reach of the bandits' clutches.

"Speaking to you as intimate friends and with the frankness that should always prevail amongst us, I say to you that as long as we remain under the influence and command of Silva, we will not be at peace, for we are always in danger of falling into the hands of the law. Therefore, it is imperative that we take care of Silva and divide his fortune equally among us. This very night he will follow his wife into eternity. That wicked old man owes numerous debts to Lucifer so he can go settle his debts with him. The crimes we have committed have repeatedly compromised us with the law, and I have had enough," the bravest of the bandits said.

The rest of the bandits answered, "What you say is true, and that is as it should be."

"If Silva kills his wife, I swear on my mother's life that I will kill him the first chance I get," said one of the fat bandits who had legs like a frog.

The bandits agreed to wait for the opportune moment to get rid of Silva. A few hours later Silva arrived with his wife whom he had met at the designated place. He sent El Lechuza to Las Vegas to assess what effect Mrs. Silva's disappearance had made.

10

JUSTICE SLEEPS

PART 1

During three years San Miguel County was overwhelmed by a chain of sinister events and horrible crimes. This would come to be known as the blackest and most disastrous period in the county's history.

First, a Turkish man by the name of Abraham Aboulafia, was murdered in his own home and his assassins remain a mystery. Sometime later, the dismembered limbs of a man, whose face was so cut up and disfigured that it was impossible to identify him, were discovered in an arroyo at the end of town. Upon closer examination, the initials "J.S." were found tattooed indelibly on his arm. Because an honest and aged tailor named "Jacobo Stuzman" had recently disappeared, a tentative identification was made. His assassins enjoyed freedom for several years until one of them—unable to ignore the voice of his conscience—turned himself and two of his accomplices in and they all paid for their transgressions.

Still later, Carpio Salas, director and treasurer of the Sabinoso Schools, disappeared. To this day his whereabouts are unknown. This unfortunate man had come to Las Vegas to pick up the money that had been appropriated to establish more public schools in his district. He received the money and that same day he was assassinated under the Gallinas River Bridge. Julián Trujillo later confessed to this crime, but to this day the body of the murdered man has not been recovered.

The numerous fires, robberies, rapes, destruction of property and other crimes and assassinations too numerous to mention gave rise to the publication of the following poem which reflected the opinion of the general public.

JUSTICE SLEEPS

Justice sleeps, and sleeps
Soothed by the lethargy of sleep,
And justice enthroned
Delights in this travesty.
It is customary but improper
To allow the criminal
To murder his victim
Out of anger or vengeance.
And to let the criminal go free
And his crime to go unpunished.

In this unlucky country
Laws are not enforced
Criminals bask in their bloody fame;
Their crimes are forgotten
And the punishment deserved
Is rarely executed.
Justice forgets the crime of murder
And laws remain forgotten.

Human life is sacred,
No one should tamper with it
Without first demonstrating
There is justification for doing so.
Defense is not forbidden,
But where chaos reigns
There is seldom an opportunity
To confer a just punishment
So, the crime will not be repeated.

So many crimes covered up!
We are aware of this.
Our own history shows us
In so many years past
How few have been punished

And the many that have been granted clemency
Rather than the deserved punishment
With the ultimate approval
That justice could confer on them.

Indifference is to blame
Creeping bias,
That one way or another
Is responsible for our ailment.
Let us do our best
To remedy these wrongs,
Forcing the criminals
To make amends before justice
For the malicious transgressions
That only cannibals are capable of.

We have witnessed without ceasing
The most horrible crimes
Performed with no excuse
Having gone unpunished.
Because the criminal is protected
By the riches he has acquired,
He uses these riches
To justify his crime
And he has always been able to do this.

The judges and the juries,
Although they are zealous citizens,
Have it within their power
To act bravely
To ensure that just punishment
Follows the commission of a crime.
In that way future evil-doing
Will be avoided,
And the just men will be honored
As true patriots.

When law is triumphant

Throughout the land,
This country will be a paradise
Of peace and tranquility
And its citizens will live without fear
And dreadful crime
Will not go unpunished,
Because powerful justice
Will be our shield and protector.

PART 2

The governor of the territory, in an effort to curtail the anomalous and untenable situation that plagued San Miguel County, expedited a proclamation offering to pardon any accomplice who would reveal the names of persons involved in crimes or assassinations committed in which the accomplice had participated. A reward of five hundred pesos was offered for each arrest and conviction.

El Mellado, with whom our readers are already acquainted, was a principal actor in many of the recent crimes. He had already been indicted by the courts for stealing cattle, and the doors of the penitentiary were wide open just waiting to receive him. El Mellado was intelligent and shrewd, however, and he realized that the governor's proclamation offered him a way of escaping his just and well-deserved punishment. At this time, he was behind bars at the county jail waiting to be tried for the crime of stealing cattle. The courts were in session and all cases were scheduled to be tried in April, 1894. In order to escape the hands of the law, El Mellado decided to inform the authorities concerning all the crimes he was aware of and in which he had participated.

Rafael Romero was the court interpreter at this time, and El Mellado reasoned that it would be an opportune time to confess to all he knew about crimes committed in the county. With the judge's and district attorney's permission, El Mellado held a conference with them on April 10, 1894. El Mellado promised to reveal everything he knew about the crimes he was aware of and had participated in on the condition that he be pardoned beforehand as promised by the territorial governor's proclamation.

Mr. Romero conferred with the judge and the attorney general and they agreed to pardon El Mellado for his crimes. Once El Mellado was convinced that they would honor their promises, he was taken before the district attorney and in his presence and that of Mr. Romero and other witnesses, El Mellado made his confession.

All men, regardless of how hardened their hearts have become, still retain a thread of sensitivity that harbors remorse. There is a dim light that shines in the darkness that can lead to the road of redemption, but it is difficult to unravel that thread. El Mellado was such a man, lacking strength and will power. Enslaved by his vices, he felt as if he was being dragged toward the abyss. He had no alternative but to confess everything or suffer the consequences. As he began his confession, he unmasked himself mercilessly. As his statement continued, the people who were present became more somber at the mention of such infamy, such terrible crimes. The men who listened attentively to El Mellado's confession were horrified.

El Mellado revealed everything, beginning with the time when the wretched gang of thieves and assassins was first organized. He told of the assassination of Patricio Maes and Gabriel Sandoval, and the plunder of Mr. Frank's store. Other assassinations had been planned, but came to naught and will not be mentioned here. El Mellado spoke slowly and provided a richness of details, often pointing to himself. No judge could have wished for more; El Mellado's confession was a deluge of revelations of terrible crimes. As he completed his confession he added in a tremulous voice: "A miserable person such as myself should cease to exist but I have a family and I beg for mercy. I love my children and my poor wife and they need me in order to survive." El Mellado's confessions are none other than have been reported in previous chapters of this book and will not be repeated here.

The following day, in accordance with El Mellado's confession, the body of young Sandoval was located in the filthy place where it had been hidden by his vile assassins. The decomposed and decaying body was exhumed in the presence of a multitude of people distressed by such a miserable and inhumane crime. Young Sandoval was positively identified by several people who had known him and he was given a decent burial.

PART 3

As a result of El Mellado's confession relative to the hanging of Patricio Maes, a judicial order was issued for the apprehension and arrest of the following persons: Vicente Silva, El Moro, El Romo, José T. Montoya (El Indio), Francisco Ulibarrí, Manuel Maldonado, Librado Polanco, Guadalupe Caballero, Procopio Rael, Nicanor Gallegos, Néstor Gallegos, Leandro Maestas, Hilario Mares, Dionicio Sisneros, Marcos Varela, Gabriel Pital and Feliciano Chávez. All these men were apprehended and arrested except for Vicente Silva, Francisco Ulibarrí, Gabriel Pital and Dionicio Sisneros, but they were being searched for eagerly. The bandits that were arrested received due process and a hearing was set.

As El Mellado was the only witness, the district attorney had to seek testimony from some of the other accomplices, and for this purpose had to offer pardons to those that chose to testify. El Romo, Lisandro Montoya, Manuel Maldonado and Hilario Mares came forward and corroborated El Mellado's testimony. The remaining bandits, upon realizing that there was no hope, surrendered to the mercy of the court. There was no need for any more witnesses for each of the accused gave a detailed account of their part in the hanging of Patricio Maes.

The court proceeded to sentence each in the following manner: El Moro, Polanco and Sisneros were sentenced to life imprisonment. Procopio Rael and Nicanor Gallegos received sentences of ten years each. Marcos Barela and Néstor Herrera were sentenced to seven years in prison. Acasio Rael and Pedro Baca received five years. Zenón Maes, who was related to the deceased, received four years in prison. José T. Montoya was sentenced to three years in prison. Such was the retribution that these wretched men received from the hands of the law.

PART 4

As mentioned previously, Vicente Silva had not been apprehended; however, the police continued to search for him, not so much in the interest of public vindication, but because a reward of one thousand five hundred pesos was offered for his arrest and conviction. This considerable sum led to unbridled greed and the so-called "detectives" and secret police looked for Silva in all the states that had received notice of the reward. Silva had been seen in several places; some people reported seeing him in Colorado, others in Wyoming and Arizona, and still others said they had seen Silva with Gabriel, Emma and Mrs. Silva in the neighboring republic of Mexico.

The people of San Miguel County expected Silva to be turned over to the authorities at any moment and there were rumors of his arrest. There was so much interest in the apprehension of this famous bandit that an individual in Pueblo, Colorado was arrested, mistakenly thinking that he was Vicente Silva. "Now it is certain," the people of Las Vegas exclaimed, "Silva is in the hands of the law." A telegraph announced the capture and arrest of Silva by a Mr. Loomis; all that was lacking was his positive identification. The necessary documents were prepared for extradition to Las Vegas, New Mexico.

A local man was sent to identify the person arrested but when he saw him he said, "You have been duped; this man is not Silva." The unfortunate man was Braulio Orono who more or less fit the description of Silva. He had been apprehended and put in jail for a few days, and now he was released. The hunt for Silva continued, but to no avail, for he could not be found. People were convinced that the earth had swallowed him.

El Mellado refused to reveal Silva's whereabouts. He said that the last time he had seen Silva was in Los Alamos on May 9 at twelve p.m. He said that he had gone to wake Silva, but Mrs. Silva had told him that Vicente was not home. On the following day neither Silva nor Mrs. Silva had been seen, and along with them, Medrán, Antonio José Valdez and Dionicio Sisneros had also disappeared. Here we will leave Silva and his wife and more will be told on this later.

11

APPREHENSION AND RETRIBUTION OF THE ACCOMPLICES
IN THE ASSASSINATION OF GABRIEL SANDOVAL

As was mentioned previously, El Mellado revealed the place where Gabriel Sandoval's body had been deposited and the body was found and exhumed. In this case, as in the case of Patricio Maes, various arrests were made even though El Mellado's testimony named only Silva as the assassin. El Mellado refused to name the accomplices but because Providence always wins out, this crime could not remain in obscurity. Guadalupe Caballero (El Lechuza) whose life was hanging by a thread as he stared into the abyss—an abyss that would cost him his life—looked for a way to save himself. Life is a precious gift and man will often sacrifice the life of another in order to save his own. Upon reflecting on his options, El Lechuza decided to pull back the veil that hid Gabriel's assassins and requested to speak to the district attorney and to the author of this book. Upon obtaining a promise that his death sentence would be reduced to life imprisonment, El Lechuza declared himself an accomplice in the assassination of Patricio Maes and Gabriel Sandoval. He also offered to reveal the details of these horrible murders. The district attorney accepted this proposition and El Lechuza gave him sufficient evidence to convict the perpetrators of these crimes.

The policemen Eugenio Alarid, José Chávez and Julián Trujillo were named as Silva's accomplices and were quickly apprehended. José Chávez escaped and was not arrested until May of 1895. The sheriff of Socorro County arrested Chávez as he was tending to some grazing sheep. Chávez was returned to San Miguel County and turned over to the proper authorities. He is awaiting trial. Alarid and Trujillo received life sentences to be served in the territorial penitentiary. On sentencing Alarid, Judge Smith spoke to him in the following way:

"Eugenio Alarid, due to the discussion of the testimony of which only the jury is aware, but which the court presumes is the jury's attempt to show mercy, your sentence has been reduced from death by hanging to accessory to a crime. Your life has been saved and the court now has the responsibility of pronouncing judgment in accordance with the jury's findings in order to ensure that you are never again in the position of taking an innocent citizen's life. Due to the indulgence of the twelve men charged with the solemn responsibility of determining your sentence and that of your accomplices, who with barbaric cruelty imposed death on your Innocent victims, nothing less than the death sentence should be imposed on you. But if the community that you have robbed and pillaged can be protected from you by sentencing you to life imprisonment, you will never again be able to threaten their peace and tranquility.

"It is not necessary for the court to describe in detail the extent of your crimes, for it is probable that your only concern is having been discovered and that justice partially, and unfortunately delayed, has finally caught up with you. However, it is imperative for the court to refer to the enormity of your crimes in order that the local citizens be made aware of the duplicity that exists in that group that should be protecting them.

You and your accomplices were selected to guard the community and to protect it from danger. In this role, you were responsible for enforcing the law and assuring the security and wellbeing of your constituents. You wore the insignia of this official duty which constituted your authority to stamp out violence and prevent crime. Your duty was to keep the community safe while it slept, to protect it against evil doers, and to guard their homes. But ignoring this sacred obligation, you became the community's enemies, yourselves the evil whom you should have rescued. Not only were you an accomplice, you became the principal conspirator. You prostituted your official position and tricked the deceased, who suspected nothing, so that you were able to lead him to the sacrifice that you knew awaited him, and finally to drag him— devastated as he was by your betrayal—to a burial place where only the devils from hell would have deposited a human being.

"Such is the account of the part you played in the tragedy and death of Gabriel Sandoval; nonetheless, out of pity, your life is spared. You should be grateful to the jury that granted you clemency and that limits the power of the law in pronouncing your sentence, which states that you should remain incarcerated in the Territorial Penitentiary for the remainder of your life."

12

ASSASSINATION OF TELÉSFORA DE SANDOVAL
AND RETRIBUTION OF VICENTE SILVA

Our readers know that Vicente Silva and Telésfora de Silva arrived at Los Alamos on the night of May 19, 1893, at a house that El Mellado had loaned them and where the rest of the gang waited anxiously. Silva ordered the bandits to leave the house as he wanted to speak privately to his wife. The gang departed and left the couple alone. Silva was very serious although he attempted to hide this as he did not want his wife to guess his intentions. Trying to appear solicitous he said to his wife:

"I am aware that you cannot ignore my situation, and because it has been necessary for me to commit some excesses of which it is too late for me to repent, I have no other alternative than to escape. Gabriel and the child are at this time at El Coyote and I am thinking of sending you there this very night so that you may be reunited with them. I have made arrangements at Fernando de Taos so that we can establish our residence there. You and the young ones can go there in a few days, but in the meantime, I must go to Las Vegas to settle some business that is pending, but I would like for you to lend me the money you have with you in case I should need it. The money that I had with me I left in Taos with orders that it be given to you."

Mrs. de Silva thought it was strange that Silva should need the small amount of money she had and, although she resisted him at first, she ended up giving him the two hundred pesos that she had. After having taken her money, Silva asked his wife to give him her gold jewelry.

Mrs. de Silva was an intelligent woman but she became suspicious when Silva requested her jewelry and said, "And why do you want my jewelry, Don Vicente? You probably want to give my jewelry to your mistress."

Silva responded, "Be quiet, woman. Seal your obscene lips."

"The truth is bitter," replied Mrs. de Silva.

"And if the truth be told, I confess that I love Flor more than I love you," said Silva.

Mrs. de Silva replied, "Well if that's the case, you are as much a criminal as you are despicable."

"And you throw my crimes in my face when you are the only person on earth that could excuse my crimes," answered Silva.

"You expect me to excuse your crimes?" said Mrs. de Silva. "No one knows you better than I, no one, and no one can so profoundly despise what you have done. You have been unfaithful to me. You have stamped on your own forehead an indelible seal of infamy. You have become a miserable bandit, an evil doer, and you never tire of inflicting suffering on me. You have dispossessed me of my money and now you want my jewelry. Don Vicente, what do you intend to do?"

"I intend to use this opportunity to my advantage and justly to punish you as you deserve," growled Silva in a menacing tone.

Mrs. de Silva was terrified and attempted to leave the room, but Silva had locked the door and she saw that her attempts to escape were futile. She exclaimed, "What do you plan to do?"

"How do you feel?" he asked.

"Don Vicente! Don Vicente! Exclaimed Mrs. de Silva.

"You know me well enough to know that I will take advantage of this instant to make you pay for all you have done," Silva said.

"Holy heaven! What are you going to do?" she screamed.

"I have already told you, I will punish you."

"Have mercy! Have mercy!" cried Mrs. de Silva falling on her knees.

"There is no mercy," said Silva.

"What did I ever do to you?" she asked.

Don Vicente pulled out a letter and said, "Get up and read."

Mrs. de Silva took the letter in her trembling hand but she could hardly hold it. She was overcome by fear, frozen by terror, for she foresaw the shadow of death. She approached the lamp and in its dim light read as follows:

Dear Don Vicente,

Your wife, Doña Telésfora, is about to push us into a bottomless pit. She has publicly revealed all of the secrets she was privy to of the crimes we have committed. This is going to cause all hell to break loose. If you want to avoid an inevitable catastrophe from falling on us see what you do with your wife. If she remains here much longer it will be much too late to remedy the situation.

Your friend,
E.A.

"Do you believe what is written in this letter? There is not a word of truth in it for I have never even imagined doing such a thing, Don Vicente. Do you think that if that were my intent I would have agreed to accompany you here? I love you, despite your faults. You are my husband," cried Mrs. de Silva.

Silva replied, "You do not love me. You are an obstinate, wicked, and evil woman."

"What dreadful words you address to a weak woman. For God's sake, do not torment me. Do you intend to kill your wife?"

"You are not my wife; you are my dishonor," Silva shouted. "Read the words in that letter; read them and be ashamed of yourself!"

Mrs. de Silva replied, "I have nothing to be ashamed of; I have nothing on my conscience. If it is a crime to follow you, or if it is a crime to stick by you, if this is unforgiveable, then kill me, but stop inventing lies. I can see that you have decided to get rid of me so that you can be with Flor. I am the obstacle in your plans."

Each time Mrs. de Silva mentioned Flor's name Silva's eyes flashed with anger and in that instant he unsheathed a dagger he had at his waist.

Seeing herself threatened, Mrs. de Silva froze and a cold sweat bathed her forehead. A mortal fear seized her as she covered her face with her hands and screamed, "My God, protect me! Save me! Soften this man's heart!"

Silva, full of wrath, angrily took his wife's arm and shook her fiercely.

Mrs. de Silva, ashen, weak and numb, her chest palpitating,

trembled with the threats of that fiend. She knew the hour of her death was approaching. Silva said, "I can read in your eyes what is in your soul. Ah, you did not expect that the husband you were about to denounce would take revenge on you. Confess that it is not an agreeable surprise." And the assassin laughed loudly as his laughter sounded like an echo from the dead in the heart of that anguished, unfortunate woman.

"Well then, let's get on with this. I do not want to seem cruel. It is more merciful to kill quickly," and after saying this he plunged the dagger in the center of her panting chest. A sea of boiling blood gushed out of the wound. Mrs. de Silva shuttered violently as her body slumped onto the hard ground.

Silva contemplated his deed for an instant as his victim writhed in a pool of blood as she lay dying. The face of that martyred woman turned pale, her eyes closed as her lips murmured a last sigh and she ceased to exist.

Silva felt satisfied for he had added another bloody page to the black history of his life. He reflected: "This is ended. If the dead could only appreciate all the favors they receive, this unfortunate woman would pardon me for what I have just done to her. I have saved her from committing the infamy of turning me in to the law, sooner or later. Now I am safe." And he walked into the next room where the other bandits awaited him.

"Hello!" said El Patas de Rana. "What is the program we should follow tonight?"

"What do I know about programs," answered Silva. "What I know is that I have gotten rid of that woman and I need your help to give her a decent burial worthy of us."

The bandits entered the room where the inert body of Mrs. de Silva was lying. Upon contemplating the scene before him El Mellado said, "How well our captain wields the dagger."

"Yes," said another bandit, "he is an expert at the art."

"What if he ever caught Captain Esquibel within range!" said El Mellado.

"I would be happy to make him dance a jig," commented Silva in a ludicrous tone, "but he will have his turn. I have him on my list. The commotion he has made over the horses belonging to his son, Refugio, will cost him dearly; I will cure him of his prudishness." Silva harbored great resentment against Capitan Esquibel for taking an active part in accusing him of stealing the horses that Esquibel' s son, Refugio, brought back from Monte Largo.

Silva unbuckled his belt and pulled it from his waistband where there was a large amount of greenbacks. The eyes of the bandits shone with pleasure at the sight. Silva gave each of the bandits ten pesos and said, "Prepare a grave for this unfortunate wretch."

He ordered the body to be wrapped in several blankets and shawls as if it were a bale of goods. Silva told the men to pick the body up and follow him as he guided them to a place called "El Campo de los Cadillos, about five thousand feet south of Los Alamos.

El Campo de los Cadillos has a level plane initially, but a short distance away there is a drop one thousand feet with numerous arroyos, some of which are twelve feet wide. Silva chose the place that seemed most suitable to hide the body of his wife and ordered that she be put into it. Then the bandits tore down both sides of the bank and Mrs. de Silva's body remained eternally covered.

Once Mrs. de Silva's burial was completed, Silva ordered the bandits to return to the house. They had barely traveled about thirty feet from the burial site when Patas de Rana, who was walking on Silva's left side, received a signal the bandits had previously agreed upon. In not more than a second he cocked his gun and fired at Silva's left temple. Silva fell to the ground as if struck by lightning and died.

13
DISTRIBUTION OF GOODS

After searching and taking the money and jewels from Silva's purse and pockets, the bandits declared themselves administrators and heirs and distributed the booty amongst themselves in a just and equitable way. There was no need to dig a grave as there was an arroyo nearby as deep as the one Silva had chosen for his wife. Without further ceremony they rolled Silva into the arroyo and buried him in the same way they had his wife by collapsing the bank on each side to cover him. The deed was done. The infamous bandit who had been the scourge and terror of San Miguel County received his just punishment at the hands of that family of demons that he himself had created and educated in his ways.

The bandits dispersed; each went his own way. El Patas de Rana appeared at dawn in El Coyote. Medrán and Sandoval went to Las Vegas; El Moro and El Mellado went to their respective homes in Los Alamos, and Dionicio Sisneros went to Watrous. The following day Sisneros borrowed a horse and carriage from a relative on the pretext of taking his family to Los Yutas. However, he left in a different direction and in a few days he arrived in Winslow, Arizona.

PART 1

The day after El Mellado's confession the District Attorney ordered the excavation of the grave site where Gabriel Sandoval had been buried. Juan Padilla and José M. Baca were put in charge of that horrible and loathsome project. Work began at nine a.m. on April 11,

1894. Within an hour the body of Gabriel Sandoval was positively identified, and several arrests were immediately made. Among these was El Menguado who not only was an accomplice in the assassination of Patricio Maes, but was aware of all the facts concerning the death of young Sandoval.

El Menguado, following the example of El Mellado, confessed to the District Attorney and to the author of this book. He revealed all the facts concerning the assassination and burial of Gabriel Sandoval. This confession brought about the immediate arrest of Julián Trujillo and Eugenio Alarid who still wore their policemen badges. José Chávez y Chávez, who had the reputation of being an expert on the subject of assassination, was at the plaza at this time, but upon hearing that he was about to be arrested, he made his escape. He sought asylum in the deserts and deserted regions of the Territory of Arizona where he remained until May, 1895. At that time, the sheriff of Socorro County found El Menguado and arrested him as he shepherded a herd of sheep grazing. El Menguado had changed his name to José Gonzales. The sheriff turned him over to the authorities of San Miguel County and he is now awaiting trial.

PART 2

The "policeman" Eugenio Alarid was named as one of the assassins of young Sandoval and was brought to trial. El Menguado and Julián Trujillo were the principal witnesses. After a week of hearings the jury returned a verdict of second degree murder. Julián Trujillo received the same verdict.

14
EVENTS NARRATED BY EL MELLADO

PART 1

On the night that young Sandoval was assassinated and buried, Silva headed to Los Alamos where El Mellado and Dionicio Sisneros lived. It was a dark, snowy night. The roads were covered with snow and Silva became disoriented and did not know where he was until the early signs of dawn appeared and he discovered that he was several miles west of Los Alamos. He then turned toward his destination and arrived there before sunrise. El Mellado came out to greet him, and Silva returned his greeting.

Silva said to his cohorts: "I waited for you last night at our pre-arranged meeting place and I do not know why you did not show up. As it turned out, however, your services were not required because the work is done. I had the good fortune of disposing of my young brother-in-law and today he is resting in a site that for many years I used as my latrine. Now I only need to settle my account with Doña Telésfora."

El Mellado wanted to hear the details of the assassination, but Silva was not about to reveal these to anyone. Silva's clothes were as bloody as a butchers and at that moment he could have instilled fear into the heart of the bravest of men. He looked like the devil himself and El Mellado—aware of Silva's character—desisted from asking any more questions.

Silva ordered that a bed be prepared for him and proceeded to attempt to get some rest for his fatigued body, but his mind was over-excited, and sleep eluded him as he re-played the bloodshed of the previous night and thought of ways to get rid of his wife. He finally decided to get out of bed and ordered that his horse be saddled. He went to El Coyote where he remained until he and his bandits devised the plan to rob Mrs. William Frank's store.

PART 2

After that Silva and his bandits hid in their lair, El Coyote. From here they carried on their raids on the surrounding areas committing all kinds of robberies. They were so brazen that they penetrated establishments on the nights when they knew were the most favorable to them. They were so greedy that they assaulted carriages and any other properties that caught their eye.

Juan de Dios and Tomás Lucero, known as "Los Cuates" (The Twins) and Sóstenes Lucero (Juan's son), were active members of Silva's gang. Silva granted them the authority to rob and pillage in certain places. Silva, as leader of the bandits, had divided the Territory into districts that could be vandalized. The counties of Mora, Taos, and Colfax were assigned to the twins, with special permission to cross over to the state of Colorado.

Los Cuates were cunning fellows who had broken the seventh commandment from the time they were young boys. Their only occupation was to steal every which way they could, for robbery was their politics, their religion, their belief, and their ambition. Both bandits had served time in the penitentiaries of New Mexico and Nebraska. Los Cuates and Sóstenes Lucero were famous thieves, but had never killed anyone until they enlisted in Silva's corrupt band. They followed Silva's example and, in order to prove their valor and skill, they proposed and carried out the assassination of Mr. John Dougherty who was an influential cattleman in Mora County. Los Cuates feared that Mr. Dougherty would prosecute them for their misdeeds. Later they killed Antonio Rael, a member of their own gang, who had helped them assassinate Mr. Dougherty. They killed him because they feared he might expose them. They are now serving life sentences in the penitentiary for these crimes.

PART 3

Silva had completed most of his planned misdeeds, but he had one more thing to do. Because of where he had sent young Emma she presented an obstacle to Silva before he could carry out the assassination of his wife. Upon reflecting on this, Silva decided to send Emma to Fernando de Taos where she would be safe while he carried out the assassination of his wife.

He took the horses that he and his bandits had stolen at great risk and left for Taos taking little Emma with him. They traveled in a carriage that had cost Silva no more than the horses. They remained in Taos only long enough to sell the stolen property; Silva then returned accompanied by El Mellado and Sisneros who had escorted him on his lucrative trip. Emma was placed in the Presbyterian Mission School in Taos.

15

ASSASSINATION OF BENIGNO MARTÍNEZ AND JUAN GALLEGOS

On May 26, 1893 the people of Las Vegas were very perturbed. They had heard that two men had been assassinated in the vicinity of Vegoso, six miles east of Las Vegas. The two men were Benigno Martínez and Juan Gallegos. Benigno raised sheep and at great personal sacrifice had been able to increase his herd to almost two thousand head. On this fateful day, Benigno Martínez and Juan Gallegos were watching the sheep graze unaware of the danger that surrounded them when Cecilio Lucero, a member of Silva's gang of bandits, attacked and killed them. These assassinations were so horrific that this pen has difficulty describing them.

Cecilio Lucero and Benigno Martínez were cousins. Cecilio and his wife lived in the Martínez home and were granted many favors as relatives and friends. Cecilio had been in Watrous the previous day and was known to be offering to sell a herd of sheep, but it is not known whether anyone accepted his offer. The following day he returned to the camp where Benigno was guarding his sheep and stayed with him overnight. The next day at dusk, with no motive whatsoever, he shot and instantly killed Benigno Martínez and with a second shot killed Juan Gallegos. Not satisfied with killing the men, Cecilio crushed their heads by pounding them with a rock. The victims were so horribly mutilated that it was difficult to identify them except for the clothes they wore and some letters they carried in their pockets that were discovered by the coroner. In order to augment even more this cold-blooded, evil assassination Cecilio folded a rope in half, tied one end to the neck of a burro, and the other end to Benigno's feet. He then turned the dead man face up and did the same to Juan Gallegos. The burro dragged the dead men around all day and into the evening.

The following day Mr. Juan Aragón was on the road to Las Vegas when he noticed a burro dragging something. Out of curiosity he went to investigate and this is what he later said: "When I saw this horrific spectacle my hair stood on end," and he hurried to town and reported what he had seen.

In a short time the officials, accompanied by a number of citizens, hurried to the scene of this terrible crime. They did not take long to return to Las Vegas with the mangled bodies which they delivered to the coroner for a post mortem examination. The excitement was general as hundreds of people gathered to see the dead men. The sight of these bloody bodies covered in dust and mud caused mass indignation and everyone clamored for vengeance.

Following an exparte examination the author of these diabolical crimes was discovered. Cecilio Lucero was apprehended and placed in the city jail. After due process and a preliminary hearing Cecilio Lucero was found guilty of the murders of Benigno Martínez and Juan Gallegos. The public was infuriated. At eleven p.m. more than three hundred people broke into the jail, took Cecilio Lucero, and hung him from a lamp post. Such was the retribution of Silva's confederate bandit.

16
GERMÁN MAESTAS: HIS MARRIAGE AND MISHAPS

Germán Maestas was a young man of twenty-six years; however, when he was just twenty years old he started out on a very gloomy path. He never attempted to perform any gratuitous act that would qualify him as a human being that feels the pangs of conscience; his instincts were aggressive and immoral, causing the police to follow his trail. Germán Maestas has several pages in the register of the criminal courts noting several convictions for robbery, one for rape, and one for murder. The prison gates were always ready to receive him. Germán's indifference was such that jail for him represented nothing more than his home or a hospital. On the day he was released from jail for serving time for some petty theft or bad behavior he addressed his jailer with the following words: "See you later," and in effect not much time transpired until he was back in jail.

Germán Maestas had been a follower of the bandit who is the principal character in this story and had learned the lesson well of taking what did not belong to him. He took pride in being a thief. He knew all the members of Vicente Silva's gang, and they all knew him. The bandits considered themselves members of the same family and helped each other on their dangerous road to infamy.

Maestas had married Rosa Durán secretly. They were married by the Justice of the Peace, Estéban Saenz, in the Los Alamos precinct. The Justice of the Peace guarded the secret of their marriage closely. The marriage was not even recorded in the register of the County Clerk as the law required.

In 1894 Maestas was jailed for two months for some transgression he had committed. His wife Rosa, left alone and without anyone knowing of her marriage, was being courted by a young man named Pedro Romero. Pedro Romero searched the public register for any record of Rosa's marriage to Maestas and having found none, proposed to her. Rosa accepted his proposal and Pedro made arrangements with El Mellado, who was Justice of the Peace at that time. El Mellado declared Rosa and Pedro legally married.

Maestas learned of the marriage while he was in jail; he still had a few days to serve on his sentence. On learning of Rosa's marriage, he went into a terrible rage. He was like a tiger in a cage wanting vengeance. Only one week was left for the completion of his sentence and the jailer gave him plenty of freedom. Maestas could not wait any longer so he made his escape and joined a young man named Montaño. After stealing some horses they hurried to Los Alamos to exact vengeance on Pedro Romero. It was late at night when they broke into Romero's residence and flogged him in a violent and merciless way. Then they tied him to a chair and left taking Rosa with them and headed for El Salitre, twenty miles away, where Maestas previously resided.

The unfortunate Pedro Romero screamed, asked for pardon, offered to give Silva, his wife, Rosa, but Maestas did not want to leave before settling accounts with Romero for imitating Mohammed and committing the crime of bigamy. That same night the group arrived at El Salitre. Silva absolved his wife of all blame and left her in the house while he left to steal some better horses before day break.

PART 1
ROSA'S ESCAPE

While Maestas was looking for horses, Rosa took advantage of her time alone and made her escape. She ran through secluded roads and finally reached the house where Pedro Romero was still tied up. Maestas returned home with his beautiful sorrel horses to find that his pigeon had flown the coop.

PART 2
PEDRO ROMERO'S ASSASSINATION

When he found that Rosa had escaped, Germán Maestas became very angry and swore vengeance. That same day he and Jesús Vialpando took off in pursuit of Rosa but could not find her. By this time the sun had set and the two men sought shelter at the edge of the Sapello River. The following morning they headed for Los Alamos. They had not traveled far when they spotted a flock of sheep grazing close by at a place called La Cejita Dulce. The men were hungry so they decided to delay their departure and eat something. As they approached the camp the dogs started barking. Maestas pulled out his gun and fired a few shots. At that point Pedro Romero stepped forward and shouted "Stop!" Not realizing that it was his arch rival and competitor that had shot at the dogs. Maestas, on the other hand—who had sharp eyes—recognized Pedro Romero immediately. On coming closer, Pedro Romero also recognized Maestas, but he was in a daze and completely paralyzed by fear. He saw that the newcomers had the advantage and were armed to the teeth. They were so threatening that they could have instilled fear in all of Napoleon's army after its retreat from Moscow.

The bandits ordered Romero to serve them breakfast and he promptly gave them what food he had. During that royal breakfast Maestas turned to Romero and sarcastically asked him: "How do you like Rosa as a wife?"

Romero trembled with fear and did not respond.

Maestas shouted, "You wretched coward! You thought you could make fun of me while I was in jail by marrying my Rosa, isn't that true?"

Romero answered, "She deceived me and..."

Maestas laughed, "Ha, ha, ha. The serpent deceived Eve and Eve deceived Adam, right! Which one of these roles would you like to play, my friend?"

Romero answered, "I do not play any role. The only script I have is the one the judge gave me when he married us."

Maestas responded, "Well, well! You should have come to the jail to find me so that I could sign as a witness. Don't you think that would have been much better? I would have handed Rosita over to you and you would have given me a receipt. And where is she now?"

"I do not know," said Romero, "You took her away the other night."

"Ah!" said Maestas. "I remember what happened now, but she escaped and I thought she would come here to be with you."

Romero was as still and silent as a statue, expecting a fatal outcome. The sarcastic remarks that Maestas shouted confused him. Here were his two formidable enemies standing in front of him and he did not know what to do. Minutes seemed like hours. Maestas, full of anger, wanted some reason to injure or kill Romero in order to satisfy his insatiable thirst for vengeance.

"I want to be rid of you," remarked Maestas. "What you have done to me is intolerable. The stain you have left on my forehead can only be washed away with blood. " Romero attempted to pull out his pistol, but Maestas and Vialpando fired simultaneously hitting Romero in the head. Romero's body fell over the fire where he had fixed the bandits' breakfast. A thirteen-year old boy witnessed the terrible crime. Maestas wanted to shoot the boy, but Vialpando stopped him. The bandits mounted their horses and abandoned their victim's body to be consumed by fire.

PART 3
ALERTING THE AUTHORITIES

As soon as the bandits were out of sight the young boy pulled the body from the fire and hurried to Los Alamos to deliver the bitter news. After leaving the site of their unspeakable crime Maestas and Vialpando separated and each went his own way. A few days later Maestas was apprehended near Lamy by Sheriff Lorenzo López and put in jail. In due time he was prosecuted for the assassination of Pedro Romero and received the maximum sentence.

PART 4
RETRIBUTION

On May 15, 1894 Germán Maestas was executed at the town gallows after being given the proper rites of the Catholic Church.

17
ASSASSINATION OF TOMÁS MARTÍNEZ

Jesús Vialpando was thirty-seven years old at the time of the treacherous assassination of Pedro Romero. He appeared not to be an evil person until his ruinous friendship with Germán Maestas and his joining Silva's gang. Once Maestas was arrested for the crime they had mutually committed, Jesús Vialpando feared the law. He ran away and remained a fugitive roaming around for some time, robbing and committing other atrocities.

In January of 1895, accompanied by Feliciano Chávez and sixteen year old Emilio Enciñias, Vialpando rode to San Pedro and sold some stolen horses. They remained in San Pedro for several days and returned to San Miguel County on February 20. On the way they stopped at a ranch belonging to Mr. Tomás Martínez. Inspired by the greed they felt for goods that were not their own, they slaughtered a steer to supply themselves with meat. While Vialpando and his companions were enjoying some choice roast meat young Tomás Martínez arrived. He had a dog with him.

The gang knew that the steer was the property of Martínez and fearing he might accuse them of stealing it, they decided to kill him. They sent young Emilio and another bird of the same species that had joined the gang in San Pedro with orders to wait for the bandits on the road. The two young men left immediately leaving Vialpando, Chávez and Martínez at the ranch. It was a bitterly cold day with more than eighteen inches of snow on the ground. The bandits had a big fire going for the forest offered them all the wood they needed. Martínez warmed himself for a moment, then left to inspect the slaughtered animal's hide.

He briefly examined the hide, then returned to the fire standing with his back to it in order to warm himself completely.

Vialpando, without any warning to Martínez, shot twice in succession. Young Martínez fell dead. Then Feliciano shot the dog who ran off howling and disappeared. But the monstrous bandits were not satisfied with killing Martínez so they laid his body over the fire and covered it with more wood. Their infamous satanic task having concluded, the bandits left to join their two companions, taking Martínez's horse with them.

18
GALLARDO GIVES NOTICE OF THE ASSASSINATION

Either chance or providence, who never lets evil to go unpunished, allowed the injured dog that constantly followed Tomás Martínez to go to the Martínez home that same day. The family noticed that the dog was injured and kept howling and jumping up and down and appeared to want them to follow him to the place where he had been injured. The dog was unable to talk, but his instinct and his mournful bark communicated to them that some misfortune had befallen young Martínez.

The place that was the site of the assassination was called "El Rancho de la Muralla." This was two leagues from the Martínez residence, but Tomás was nowhere to be found. His family was getting worried and as they became more fearful they could not understand why Tomás and his dog were separated. The dog followed Tomás Martínez everywhere and as they approached their home the dog would normally run ahead and let everyone know that Tomás was right behind him. But this day was different. Gallardo (this was the dog's name) came to notify the family that Tomás had succumbed to the bullets of two miserable bandits.

Gallardo was an extraordinary dog. His instincts were more acute than those of any other animal of that species. It is frequently said that a dog is man's best friend. He guards the home while his owner sleeps. He barks at strangers and loves his master. The dog also has noble sentiments: he becomes sad when his master or a family member is hurt. He howls, and his howl is more tragic, more moving, and sadder than man's sorrow. With his mournful moan Gallardo was communicating to the family that something terrible had happened to his young Tomás and that they should go in search of him. Gallardo ran on ahead of the family, continuing to moan, and led them to the spot where the fire was already extinguished. Nothing but ashes were visible. Members of the family looked around but did not find anything that indicated that the ashes were those of Tomás. All that they saw was what remained of the steer the bandits had slaughtered.

Gallardo howled and circled the ashes where once the fire had burned. The searchers were ready to give up when Gallardo started digging in the ashes with his paws and pulled out a fragment of a leg that contained part of a shoe. This was identified by the search party as belonging to Tomás Martínez. Imagine the surprise of those who had not yet lost hope of finding Tomás alive. Since the weather was quite cold they believed that young Martínez had become numb or was warming himself close to the mountain. They began to dig among the ashes and found more of the remains that had once been Tomás Martínez.

PART 1
INVESTIGATIONS

The news of this horrific assassination spread through all parts of the Territory. Young Martínez had many relatives and many friends and they began of look for clues that might have led to his assassination. They discovered many clues that pointed to the perpetrators of this inhumane crime.

The hoof prints of four horses indicated that the bandits had left El Rancho de la Muralla and headed for a village called Las Mulas. The hoof prints showed that Vialpando, Chávez and two other men had arrived at that village on the day of the crime, but disappeared at nightfall of that same day. The bandits' identities were finally established. The officers and detectives, by means of cleverly contrived tricks, tried to outwit the outlaws. The officials and detectives devised a strategy by which they convinced Emilio, who had been with the bandits, to accompany them to Rowe on the pretext of giving him a job. Once there Emilio was interrogated and he confessed that they had stolen a cow and had an encounter with Tomás Martínez.

PART 2

APPREHENSION OF VIALPANDO AND FELICIANO CHÁVEZ

On February 5, 1895 Sheriff Hilario Romero and Daniel C. de Baca arrested Feliciano Chávez in Los Valles de San Agustín. That same night Chávez confessed to all the particulars of the crime. He also told his interrogators that they could find Vialpando in La Tablazón. Early next morning Sheriff Romero, accompanied by the sheriff of Santa Fe County, surrounded Vialpando's house and arrested him.

The two offenders were turned over to the sheriff of Santa Fe County and taken to the capital of the Territory where they were indicted. The jury that heard the case found them guilty of Murder in the First Degree. The court sentenced them to be executed on November 19, 1895.

PART 3

THE EXECUTION

The day for the execution was assigned as was customary. A guard watched over the two monsters on the night prior to the execution. He reported that Vialpando slept only one hour and Chávez slept three. The two men were frightened and refused breakfast the next morning.

At six a.m. the official Cunningham accompanied by deputies Romero and Hubble arrived at the prison where the convicts were. A priest came with them. He tried to prepare the prisoners to face death with resignation and courage, but both men were emotionally disturbed and could hardly speak for sobbing. They were pale as death. Their time was up and they had to repay blood with blood. The men handed Sheriff Romero $3.25 each, donations they had gathered in prison. They asked the Sheriff to give the petty amounts to their wives who were about to become widows.

The official announced that everything was ready for the execution. Vialpando turned pale and trembled at hearing the terrible news. He went to the crucifix he had brought with him and sobbing he kissed it repeatedly. He murmured his goodbye and lowering his eyes said, "I am ready."

Vialpando was immediately escorted by carriage to the scaffold that had been built just outside the city. Many people had gathered to witness the execution of the two prisoners. Vialpando felt faint and could hardly stand upright; the officers had to help him up the fatal steps of the platform. After the executioners placed a black hood over his head the rope around his neck was tightened. The trapdoor was opened with a loud and terrifying noise and Vialpando fell dead instantly.

Immediately following the same retinue of executioners that had put an end to Vialpando's life according to the law returned to the prison where Feliciano Chávez awaited his turn. Upon entering the cell they found Chávez on his knees, praying, and without waiting for his executioners to speak he stood up and said, "Let's go; I am ready." A sepulchral silence reigned during those moments. Chávez held a crucifix in his hands which he kissed constantly. Chávez knelt before Sheriff Romero and said, "Don Hilario, I am resigned and ready to die like a man, to suffer as I deserve. This is what my Creator wishes. "Still on his knees he begged the sheriff to give him his blessing.

After such a moving scene the executioners put Chávez in a carriage and escorted him to the scaffold. At 7:40 a.m. the prisoner climbed on to the platform without any help and although Chávez was just as emotional as Vialpando had been; he demonstrated more fortitude at the hour of his death. He stood firmly on his feet and with the executioner's permission, he spoke a few words. Some of the things he said were that he had been a good citizen, a good son, a good husband and father, but because he had gotten caught up with bad companions, he was condemned to death before his time. He cautioned parents to keep their children away from bad company because he realized too late how far he had strayed from virtue. He continued: "May it be God's will that the shedding of my blood on this scaffold will serve as an example to society so that the killing will end with me."

Chávez's observations having concluded a black hood was placed over his head and the rope was put on his neck. He continued shouting "Goodbye, my friends. Have mercy!" Then the trapdoor was opened and Feliciano Chávez ceased to exist. The law was vindicated. The prisoners' dead bodies were turned over to their wives to be prepared for burial.

19

THE THISTLE CAMP

The search for Silva and his wife continued more intensely than ever, but to no avail. The author of this account had taken a great interest in unraveling these tragic events, and through his efforts it was discovered that Silva and his wife had been assassinated. Dona Telésfora de Silva had been killed by Silva, and Silva had died at the hands of his bandit gang. Medrán related all the details related to the assassination of Mrs. de Silva of which our readers are already aware. Medrán also revealed that Vicente and Mrs. Silva were buried in the Thistle Camp (El Campo de los Cadillos).

On March 17, 1895, the Silvas' bodies were exhumed and brought to Las Vegas. After proper identification, Mrs. Silva was buried in the Catholic cemetery; Vicente Silva was buried in an unobstructed plain; since everyone knew how he had conducted himself in life and the numerous crimes he had committed, no one mourned him. Sadly, his name continues to be infamous, and writers describe him as an abominable monster whose evil and wicked way no one dares to defend.

As for Flor de la Peña, suffice it to say that since the unraveling of the events we have just narrated, she has amended her ways and is trying to regain her reputation. People now look on her with compassion, and she is considered an unfortunate woman rather than a criminal.

20
The Honorable Lewis C. Fort

The attorney who with great success contributed to the discovery of the aforementioned crimes is L.C. Fort, who had been living in Las Vegas for fifteen years. His diligence, perseverance, and ability led him to apprehend and present before the law bandits and assassins and to disband criminal organizations that had existed for such a long time in the County of San Miguel and neighboring counties. During his incumbency he has been recognized as one of the most prominent lawyers of the Territory.

Mr. Fort came to Law Vegas from Little Rock, Arkansas in the year 1880. He practiced his profession in Arkansas before arriving in New Mexico at the age of fifty. During his stay in the Territory he served as District Attorney for San Miguel, Mora, Guadalupe, and Union Counties.

During Mr. Fort's tenure as District Attorney he was more successful in his prosecutions than any other official in the Territory, having convicted more criminals and lost fewer cases than any other prosecutor, as shown by the district's court archives. He is deserving of the applause and approval of the good citizens of the Territory and should be credited for establishing peace and securing the protection of the community due to his energy and capability with which he has performed these tasks.

Mr. Fort was born in Baltimore, Maryland. His service during the civil war was with Company D in the tenth regiment of Maryland. At the conclusion of the civil war in 1865 he went to the state of Arkansas where he practiced law until 1880. He then moved to New Mexico where he has lived ever since. Mr. Fort has been honored by the citizens of San Miguel County, having been elected twice to the Legislature of the Territory. He was a member of the Legislature until 1879. He served as council in 1879 and was elected to the Senate in 1887. In both cases he performed his duties with dignity gaining the approval and appreciation of his constituents.

During his tenure as a member of the Legislature and up until the present date Mr. Fort has been a strong and consistent supporter of the public education system in the Territory of New Mexico. He is in large part deserving of the public's gratitude for the existing laws. Later on as District Attorney of the city of Las Vegas he performed his duties honorably during several terms utilizing his influence as a member of the city council. He was also responsible for the construction of the beautiful building dedicated to public instruction that now adorns our city. This is the first building that has been constructed in the Territory by directly taxing the citizens and serves as an example to stimulate other communities to support and maintain their public schools. The building is also a monument to the people who contributed to its construction as well as to the illustrious lawyer who came up with the idea of constructing such a building.

21

SUPERIOR JUDGE THOMAS SMITH

To honor those who deserve it is an obligation that applies to every person with feeling. The struggle between law makers and law breakers places an obligation on the officers of the law and on most of the offenders that is greatly disagreeable. Valor and self-confidence are required to suppress crime; however, there are a few officials who adhere strictly to their duties, and these deserve praise. Judge Smith's supreme efforts to punish criminals and suppress crime compels us to add a few more words to our tale, not only to do him justice but also so that the people of this town will recognize and be grateful for his efforts. Judge Smith pledged to exterminate crime and reestablish the tranquility which had been lost for so many in this county.

Our readers know from the events formally narrated that José Chávez y Chávez, one of the assassins in the murder of young Gabriel Sandoval, has been in prison awaiting his fate. During the process of writing this story, the defendant was indicted on the first week of June. The case was completed in three days. The evidence was the same as that presented in the case of Eugenio Alarid. Julián Trujillo, who had previously been serving a life sentence in the Territorial Penitentiary, received an executive pardon in exchange for his testimony that was used against Chávez y Chávez. Antonio José Valdez, a treacherous thief and member of Silva's gang, was also indicted and sentenced to three years in the penitentiary.

While sentencing Chávez y Chávez, Judge Smith narrated his unspeakable deeds and spoke in this manner:

"José Chávez y Chávez, your own confession has convicted you of a crime that would have terrified the most ferocious hyenas who would have never dared approach the hole where you deposited the dead body of the unfortunate Gabriel Sandoval. Because of you and your accomplices a human being was assassinated, and his cadaver hidden in a latrine whose offensive stench provided you with protection. Shielding yourself and with total indifference to your brutality, you proceeded in your natural course as if your hands were without blemish; nevertheless, your hands were stained with the blood of the body that you consigned to pollution, and you rejoiced in the delusion that the security of your position as a policeman gave you the right to commit such a crime. You continued to dishonor the insignia of your office as if that were sufficient to seal the history of your crime. But graves give up their dead, and even while you were boldly sporting the badge which you violated and disgraced, the mystery of your crime was revealed. Although the victim was exhumed, there was silence for a while, but we believe that you were trembling with guilt. As you calmly observed the cadaver, you continued on your way, forgetting that the dead man's spirit was following you. And when the tragedy came to light you were compromised as being in league with the most detestable of the devils. Being fully aware of your guilt, you fled the community that you had abused and for some time—in full view of this temple of justice—you evaded and challenged your arrest by the authorities. You immediately set out for foreign lands, but fortunately you were too slow and you were apprehended for the vindication and security of the population of San Miguel County.

As a fugitive, you confessed that you were an accomplice with other bandits who, through lies and deception, met with the unfortunate victim and delivered him to Vicente Silva. As a fugitive, you confessed to have helped Silva consummate the fatal assault. As a fugitive, you confessed that you placed your victim's weak body in the hands of captain Silva upon which he stabbed him repeatedly in order to extinguish the last bit of life from him, if any was left. As a fugitive, you confessed to have been one of the group of men that carried the victim's body, not to give him a Christian burial, but to submerge him in a place where no human being had ever lain. As a fugitive, you confessed that you gathered additional excrement and placed it on the victim's body in order to make doubly sure that he was well hidden. As a fugitive, you confessed that upon completing your task you returned to the saloon where you had met with the unfortunate victim, pretending to be his friend by complimenting him. You then left the saloon with the young man and renewed your conspiracy plan, drinking of the same poison by which your victim became inebriated and became an easy captive for your temptations. As a fugitive, having served as a policeman, you confessed that you are a criminal and that you have broken the law. Because you are a confessed assassin guilty of the most horrendous crime known to man the law should invent a slow torture in order to punish you and you should be denied the right to a decent burial. But the law punishes in a just manner those who violate it, and all the ceremony due to a solemn execution will be granted to you.

Having been convicted by a jury of your peers of Murder in the First Degree for your participation in the assassination of Gabriel Sandoval the law decrees that said crime must be punished by death and you are sentenced to be hanged by order of the District Attorney of San Miguel County. This sentence will be carried out between the hours of ten a.m. and four p.m. on July 10, 1896."

Judge Smith, on becoming Superior Judge and Judge of the Court of the District of San Miguel, found that the people of this county were troubled by the large number of heinous crimes being committed. These crimes, although wrapped in mystery, came to light because of Judge Smith's persistence in demanding the most rigid and rigorous adherence to the law and his emphatic appeals to juries urging them to comply with their duties. In a short time, he was successful in restoring a sense of security to everyone and protection of their property. Judge Smith left nothing undone that was within his power to ameliorate on behalf of the suffering people. He is responsible for the improvements to our temple of justice. He has made himself personally responsible in overseeing that the public buildings of our county are conserved in a state of decency and cleanliness. Under his counsel and direction, the county treasury is recovering its assets, and the economic system established by Judge Smith is envied by his enemies.

Judge Smith is one of the most distinguished citizens of the Territory. As an official and as a private person he has upheld his duties and the history of his devotion to his official obligations should be a source of inspiration. Today Judge Smith is a leader of the legal profession, not only in New Mexico but in the entire nation.

Judge Smith was born in Culpepper County in the state of Virginia on July 26, 1838. His father, William Smith, descended from two prominent families: the Donaphins and the Smiths. The Donaphins descend from the Spaniards and the Scots and have occupied important positions including a judgeship of the Supreme Court and representative in the National Congress.

Judge Smith was educated in Washington, DC. Upon graduating from William and Mary College he decided to study law, enrolling in a law program at the University of Virginia and later in West Virginia. When the Civil War broke out he enrolled in the Kanawha Rifles, but was later named Major in the thirty-sixth Regiment of Virginia. He was successful in some skirmishes with the federal forces, and was promoted and commissioned as Brigadier General shortly before the Evacuation of Richmond.

Upon conclusion of the War Judge Smith retired to private life, living in Fauquier County where he practiced law. In 1872 he was elected as state legislator for Fauquier County and gained popularity for his financial astuteness and for his efforts to settle Virginia's debt. In 1884 President Cleveland named him United States Procurator for New Mexico and in 1892 he was named Superior Judge of New Mexico. He occupies that post to this day and has fulfilled his duties to the complete satisfaction of the people of the Territory. He has sentenced evil doers in a way commensurate with the enormity of their crimes and these sentences have been a warning to would-be criminals.

22
CONCLUSION

We conclude by saying that as long as evil-doers live alongside men who enjoy liberty and bear responsibility for their actions, the hope of ignoring the rigors of the law will never be abandoned. Nevertheless, the existence of these criminals is troubling, fraught with sudden assaults and fears. Their sleep is unsettled, they imagine danger where it doesn't exist. They conjure a vision of an extended arm always ready to capture them. Anyone who looks their way frightens them, they believe that every spoken word is an accusation, they are always on edge and their conscience makes them insecure. If the law apprehends them, if these men are put in prison, if the end of their lives resides on the scaffold for capital punishment, then it is too late to repent of their wrong doing.

It is rare and practically impossible for a criminal who has fallen into the hands of the law to save himself for it is difficult to fool judges, especially if the crime is one of some importance. The law digs, questions, and looks and finally identifies the crime and the criminal and he is punished.

From heaven to hell, from opulence to misery, from wellbeing to the discomfort of the jail cell, no one ever undergoes these troubles with a smile on his face and happiness in his heart; instead, his head is full of tempestuous thoughts, his spirit is perturbed and his heart is filled with anguish.

Oh! If men only understood the anguish that wrong doing costs them, the tragedy and the terror that it brings, this world would be a society of angels, and these unfortunate ones whose names are listed on these pages, would never have touched the hand of death or of prison. But man is incorrigible and lives his life in search of happiness without ever finding it, and counseled by his passions, dominated by his vices and by his association with bad companions, he finally arrives at the doors of death or prison, filled with remorse, and remembers when it is too late what he did and what he might have done during his past life, and on surrendering his liberty he leaves behind a sad memory: his children, his wives, his parents drowning in the memories of his disgrace, whose legacy is only tragedy and the tears of his unlucky family.

Milton Keynes UK
Ingram Content Group UK Ltd.
UKHW051647220324
439940UK00004B/254

9 781632 933706